NO MORE TIES...

BUT WILL THERE BE DONUTS?

Jerry Della Rocca

Antemortem Books
New York MMXII

Dedication

To my Funseekers – the opportunity to provide you with a reason to smile has given my "second career" meaning.

To the love of my life, who encouraged me to accept the "early retirement offer," when I had no idea what the future would hold for us. Since then she has been completely supportive of all of my career pursuits.

CONTENTS

Introduction

Cradle to grave employment – many baby boomers grew up thinking this was their birthright. But what happens when the employment bough breaks? Is there a welcoming hammock or hard-baked clay beneath?

With many of that generation being confronted with "early retirement," contending with these questions can be very stressful. That is, unless you can find happiness and humor in the various steps taken in the pursuit of a happy resolution.

After a career of more than thirty years with the same company, I was encouraged to accept an early retirement offer and explore the answer to what lies beneath the cradle.

Electing to view my life as it is, a veritable "bowl of cherries," I have chronicled my search for the ideal second career in a series of essays. As you will discover, most of my days have found the hammock, though it often has a hole or two in it. May these stories help you to find the hammock that may rest just above your set of rocks.

The Beginning

The beginning of my "next career" has finally arrived. With the singing of Auld Lang Syne and downing that last piece of rum-laced fruit cake, it was now time to face "the first day of the rest of my life."

The last several weeks were too much like vacation. With preparations for the year-end holidays and hosting numerous family and friends, I had little time to think about my new status in life. Today, however, that all changed. I would formally commence the search for that which will be my livelihood until I elect to truly retire.

Habit rousted me from a deep slumber, though about an hour later than usual. Rolling over to comment on the blessed absence of the annoying alarm I found that my bed co-habitant was missing as well.

As the full impact of this momentous day slowly sank into my still groggy mind, the sweet aroma of freshly perked French Vanilla coffee wafted into the room. Resisting the urge to follow its siren-like call I headed instead to a long, luxurious shower and shave.

Half an hour later, enshrouded in a cologne fog, I entered the kitchen in search of my love. This was to be the classic breakfast together in our sun-drenched kitchen (though it was cloudy outside); the kind so often portrayed in those romantic coffee commercials. The aforementioned vanilla fragrance having filled my nostrils, I imagined that my love had had the same vision.

But no, this is reality. The coffee was waiting, yet my mate was in the den grunting along with some exercise video. Hmm, might this have been what I had been missing all those years when I trekked off to work each morning, or was this a New Year's resolution?

Ever the chivalrous one, I called down to her, "Honey, how about I get you some breakfast – maybe something hearty to offset that big workout?"

Her reply, interspersed with gasps of air, came as she trotted up the steps, using a towel to wipe her brow. "No thanks... I have to take a quick shower and then have to run... Have an early appointment with a client." She then disappeared down the hallway.

So much for the Nescafe' moment...

It was only then I recalled a conversation that we had had a number of times over the last few weeks. I was embarking on a new career. She was not. My partner in life had built a successful consulting business over the last two decades and was very content with it. Though I may be "in transition," she was not and, as such, asked that I respect her routine.

Glumly returning to the kitchen, I poured myself a cup of java and mulled over my new state in life.

Knowing that routine is important, I was intent on creating a good one for this time of change. Recalling that major decisions should never be tackled on an empty stomach, the first revision would begin with breakfast.

Previously, a glass of juice wolfed down as I rushed out the door would tide me over for the hour it took to reach work and my first cup of coffee. Now I had the luxury of time. I envisioned several eggs over easy, accompanied by four slices of ham and toast heavily slathered with butter – a real lumberjack's breakfast.

But then, reality struck. Such a daily surge in cholesterol would cut short the time I had to decide what to do with the rest of my life. Besides, the South Beach Diet, which I had begun at the same time I joined the ranks of the unemployed, frowned on the carb-laden toast. No, a simple bowl of high fiber cereal and a large cup of coffee would have to suffice.

Sitting alone at the table I experienced my first bit of nostalgia. I thought of Mahmud, manning his little coffee truck parked outside my office building. No longer would I casually ask for "the usual," smiling at the others in line at my elite status of *regular customer*. Of course, he would also no longer reply, "Cream and sugar?" To which I would quietly whisper, "No, you remember, black with a 'Sweet and Low'." (Though I always felt a bond usually reserved for lifelong friends, Mahmud never quite seemed to reciprocate that level of intimacy.)

I think a tear may have landed in my coffee cup.

But then, like a rush of fresh air, Elise came in to bid me farewell. "I'm off to my meeting." Following a quick peck on the cheek, she continued, "Good luck on your job search. Hope your day goes well."

As I turned to reply she was already on her way down the stairs, yelling back, "Love you!" And then she was out the door.

3

Resigning myself to what I anticipated to be a long day, I rose from my reverie and headed down to my soon-to-be christened office (previously known as the toy room).

Settling onto the folding chair that rested in front of the PC, I moved the mouse to wake the computer from its slumber. The screen lit up – with a request for a password. Hmm, this was new, though knowing the love of my life and her penchant for security, I should not have been surprised.

Just hitting the ENTER key did not work. I then typed in *PASSWORD*, and several variations of it, but all to not avail. Reaching the end of a short fuse, I picked up the phone to call the love of my life.

Failing to reply to her greeting, I jumped right in, "Honey, what's the password for the stupid computer?"

"Oh, sorry about that, knowing that young kids would be playing in the toy room I secured the computer to keep them from messing it up on you.

"Just type in the first initials of each of the kids," pausing, knowing my typing skills are not the best, "then put in the middle two numbers of my social security number..."

At which point I jumped in, "Whoa, I barely know mine, what is yours again?"

She rattled off the full nine digits, leaving it to me figure out the middle two. "Okay, I think I have it."

But no, we were not yet done; she continued, "Lastly, put in the year we were married. That should do it."

Doing so, the screen came alive and I bade her farewell.

Next came what every good desk jockey does upon arriving at the office – I logged on to the Internet. The first stop was a sports website to read several recaps of the same ballgames I had so intently watched yesterday. Someday I will decipher my purpose in this daily routine. It's a bit like watching reruns on TV – perhaps there was something I missed, that single action or word that would make the whole experience more valuable.

The silence in the house was deafening. Oh, to only hear the Xerox machine chugging out copies one more time...

Rather than allow myself to slip into more nostalgia, I decided to approach this "first day" like so many similar days on new assignments – I would set up the office.

First, those pictures of Snow White and Pooh Bear had to come down from the walls. Next, a miniature steel drum, brought back from our honeymoon well over thirty years ago, had to come off the table that was now to be my desk. These would be replaced by the more professional accoutrements that had followed me from office to office over the years.

Heading to the garage, I retrieved a box that had lain dormant since my last day of work. Out came a fifteen year old photo of the kids (it helps me remember them at ages when I still felt needed). Next was a beer stein from the Red Cross labeled "Thanks for a pint"– lacking a proper desk with a drawer, it will hold pens and pencils.

Suddenly I noticed the screen on the PC had gone black. Hmm, assuming it had just gone to sleep, I moved the mouse, fully expecting it to resume its previous screen. But instead, I was faced with the infamous request for a password. Oh no.

I recalled that it began with the kids' initial letters, but then there was some part of Elise's social security... I had better just call her and get it again. (Undoubtedly, she'll say I should've written it down, but who knew I would need it again?)

My call went directly to her voicemail.

I returned to setting up the office; must stay focused.

Assuming the positions previously held by Snow White and Pooh went two remnants of days gone by. An anniversary gift clock from the company was first, followed by a framed picture of the co-ed softball team on which I was a slow-footed left fielder.

A fancy pen holder engraved with my name will enable visitors (?) to my new office to get the spelling of my name correct. Then a paper-weight statue of Snoopy playing tennis – it always added a touch of humanity to otherwise sterile office environments. Ah yes, the familiar ambience of *the office* was gently wrapping itself around me.

Then the phone rang. How shall I answer? For years, while at the office, I would answer, "Jerry Della Rocca speaking; how may I help you?" Would that be too formal here? Though, a mere "Hello" seemed so inadequate for my new surroundings.

The phone rang again. Umm, how to answer it...

Following the third ring, I picked it up, "Jerry Della Rocca speaking," only to be interrupted with, "My, my, aren't we being a bit formal." It was the love of my life. "What's up? You called?" she continued.

Forgetting for a moment what I had called about, my eyes fell upon the blank screen. "Oh, yeah, I need the password again. The stupid PC went dark and when I woke it up it was there again."

"Oh yes, I had it go to sleep if it hadn't been used for thirty minutes. I didn't want it left on while the kids were visiting.

Hmm, guess you're not being very productive on the old job search?"

"No, wise guy, I had moved my energy to making this environment a bit more professional. The only job I was going to find with Snow White watching me would entail a move to Orlando!"

"Okay, here is the number, but write it down this time." (Ah, she is just too predictable.)

She then rattled off the fourteen digit alphanumeric code. Gosh, wonder if Fort Knox is so well protected?

"Any other codes I should be aware of before I let you go? Is there a new combination lock on the refrigerator?"

"Look, I haven't got time for fooling around. I am with a client.

Also, I won't be home for lunch. We'll be grabbing something here and then I'm off to another site. I'll see you tonight." And I was left with a dial tone.

Hmm, lunch? Nah, even for me it was too early. Wonder if we still have some of those Christmas cookies upstairs?

Where was I? Ah yes, I needed to wake up the PC. Following my hastily scratched note, I typed in the digits my love provided, only to have the screen return the message, "Incorrect password." Drat!

I punched in the letters and numbers again, but got the same response! I angrily banged the table with my right fist, causing poor Snoopy to plunge to the floor separating his head from the rest of his body. Darn, that little guy has been with me a long time.

Returning to the stupid PC, with carefully placed, and increasingly heavy, strokes of the keys I input the code provided by Elise. Failure again!! But this time, I noticed that there was an extra light near the top of the keyboard. Close examination revealed that it was telling me I had activated the CAPS LOCK.

Oops. Striking that key and then gently inputting the proper code brought the computer to life, though I had forgotten what I was going to do there.

Glancing at the clock, I saw that it was slightly askew. Rising from my chair, I walked over to straighten it. It is important to periodically get up from your desk and walk around – I recalled being told that at one of my company physicals. And, of course, watching the clock was important, since I did not want to miss lunch.

About eleven o'clock my productivity followed the course of my sugar levels – it took a severe nose-dive. Probably due to the fact that I had not taken the usual mid-morning coffee break. Some of those Christmas cookies would go so well...

Instead, I pondered what the rescuing meal would be like in my new environs. No longer would I run up to the cafeteria and have one of the lunch ladies put together a tasty little salami, provolone, lettuce, tomato and roasted pepper hero. (Ah, with extra vinegar and oil...) I was on my own. I wondered what leftovers were in the fridge.

But no, I had work to do. Returning to the task at hand, I pulled financial texts, old notebooks, and binders of recent projects from the boxes. Postponing a judgment of their value, they found their way to shelves near my desk. Some old organization charts got dumped, as well as a *Forbes* article on the problems associated with the "upcoming" Y2K.

Ah, my self-discipline in continuing this arduous task was gratifying.

One minute past noon found me at the counter in the kitchen, heating some of yesterday's lasagna in the microwave. Hmm, this might not be so bad after all.

By two o'clock I was back at my desk, newly refreshed and ready to resume setting up the office. However, several emails had arrived during my time away and I felt they had to be read prior to the resumption of my labors.

Photos attached to an email from one of the kids reminded me of the last few weeks. I was pleased to see that the cameras, some of which were Christmas gifts, had been put to good use. Oops, that one of me with a "virus" on New Year's morning is not a pretty one – must remind them of the importance of "filtering" before sending out pictures.

By the time I finished replying to many of the electronic missives, and forwarding several jokes I had received in the morning, I noted that my office was becoming a bit gloomy.

With winter's early onset of dusk, I recognized another change from my old office. No longer was I enshrouded by the unfailingly flickering fluorescent lights and a magnificent view of Bryant Park. My new office did indeed have a window-view,

9

albeit of the back deck, but the lighting is limited to a small Mickey Mouse lamp – a remnant of the previous use of the room.

With the setting sun and lack of more substantial lighting, I was now literally, as well as figuratively, "working in the dark."

Flicking on Mickey's light, I saw that it was almost four o'clock. That raised another issue – what was an appropriate quitting time? After all, I did not want to set dangerous precedents for my new routine. Having spent too many late nights at the office in the past, I was determined not to continue that trend. Hmm, wonder what Elise has planned for dinner? Perhaps I should call her.

Ah, better yet, I'll pop open a bottle of wine and greet her return with a freshly poured goblet of the nectar of the gods. "Cocktail hour" – the mere sound of it is refreshing. What better way to relax and regroup after the taxing day we had both just finished? Yes, I think that is a good new ritual. As I said earlier, routine is important in our lives.

Tomorrow I will attack the search for my next career with renewed vigor.

Now, where is that bottle of Cabernet that we got for Christmas?

Passion

Shuffling into the kitchen for breakfast, I noted that the day was not very sunny; indeed, there were snowflakes blowing past the large glass sliding doors separating the kitchen from the back deck. Last night's snowfall had left a considerable amount of the white stuff on the yard, and a heavy wind was piling it into rapidly growing drifts along the fence. Boy, was I glad I would not have to venture out into that mess!

The outdoor thermometer showed the temperature to be in the teens; though, after years of slogging through such weather I knew the wind would make it feel much closer to zero! Gazing out at the last remnants of the storm, I recalled countless mornings walking to the train station during similar conditions. The bitter wind hitting me square in the face. The ache that would develop across my shoulders from hunching over to keep whatever body warmth I had inside my coat. The sensing of snow sneaking its way above my socks and freezing what little hair remained on my calves...

Ah, no more of that long, energy-draining commute. The trek from the kitchen to my new "office" is short and heated.

Following another unsatisfying breakfast of fibrous oats and too-strong coffee, I made my way to my "desk" and fired up the computer. Today was to be the day that I truly began the search for my next career. The work on what was to be my office, until I find an alternative source of employment, was sufficient for now. Not quite ready for subleasing to others, at least one would have to strain to find the *Monopoly* game. I had gotten a good night's rest. I was ready to commence the search for my passion in life.

No, I wasn't planning on spending the day looking up porn on the Internet. Rather, that is how the "early retirement" pamphlets, provided by my former company prior to leaving, portrayed my next career endeavor. According to the experts, my quest was to be, "a search for the passion that has been suppressed throughout one's life while consumed by the drudgery of work."

Except that I neither viewed my career as drudgery nor have I suppressed any passions – other than those jump-started by the *Victoria's Secret* commercials. Nevertheless, I felt it important to follow their advice – after all, I assume those pamphlets were written by H.R. professionals.

Since circumstances dictated that it was time for me to pursue another livelihood, it was time to find if I did indeed have any hidden passion. Then, I could find that company with whom I would commence a mutually beneficial second career to satisfy that suppressed drive.

It's not like I was approaching the search without a wealth of offered advice. For the past month, along with the onslaught of visiting family and friends, came a deluge of words of guidance on how to handle this latest step in my life.

My neighbor, Phil, always chasing the latest hot stock tip, told me that my future lay in day trading. "With your financial background, you could make a quick killing and retire again in another year!" Great, just what I needed – a suggestion that would not provide a career, but merely a postponement of my dilemma for twelve months. And that assumed I was successful. He obviously was not aware of my forays into the world of investing. My modus operandi was: *Buy high and then sell the day after the headlines read:* STOCK MARKET DROP SETS RECORD! I quickly discounted his input.

There was an aunt who felt that I would be good in college admissions – "You have a nice rapport with young people." Unfortunately, her opinion was based solely on that which she witnessed at family gatherings over the years. She should have seen me deal with those darlings of the Big Apple with whom I shared the sidewalks – most such contacts ended with my muttering, "Get a job!"

Those under the age of thirty directed me to online Internet search engines. "Forget the want-ads in the newspapers. Those are so Eighties! Just go to the monster and you'll have a job in no time!" (I subsequently found this to be *Monster.com*, a huge employment website.) Of course, most of those providing such counseling were either in graduate school, staying at home raising a family, or just plain unemployed!

And, lastly, there were those who had obviously suppressed their passion for a life of relaxation and hoped to enjoy it vicariously through me. They recommended a total lifestyle change – "Move south." Thoughts of a wardrobe consisting of black knee socks with white boat shoes, loud plaid (is that redundant?) Bermuda shorts and pastel-colored golf shirts came to mind. "Get yourselves a little condo and live life to the fullest! Heck, if you have to, you can always pick up a job at *Walmart* as a greeter!" The lure of warm weather was indeed appealing. But each time the "move south" proposal came up it met with a glare from the love of my life. "That whole lifestyle is an egg timer ticking off the days to the collection of your final pension check! Don't expect me to join you!"

With so much valuable advice, how could I not feel well-armed to begin my search?

No longer was my career being steered by hidden corporate HR personnel. Nor was I restricted by a need for a salary that would be sufficient to put six kids through college, while simultaneously paying down a mortgage to put a roof over their heads. I was free to pursue the passion I had suppressed for so long!

I was free at last! Yes, free at last to follow the dream that had been pent up inside for so many years!

Except, there was nothing pent up inside (other than some heartburn from the pepperoni pizza I downed while watching the football game last night). I had not been stifling any great urges to do anything else over the last few years. My life had been quite happy as a matter of fact. Nevertheless, this latest day of my next career would be spent on the hunt – searching for that which would provide me the satisfaction of the aforementioned passion.

The Internet, I was convinced, held the answer. The last few years I have learned that everything could be found out in cyberspace. I just needed to find the right keywords.

But no, I must hold back. Prior to seeking that which will satisfy me, I must take a more disciplined approach to the search for what turns me on. Uh, make that, the search for that which I have a passion.

Seeking something to bolster my confidence, I turned to my email. Perhaps someone from the old department needs help. (I had widely circulated my home email with an offer to help "post-retirement.") Maybe I'd find a question about the preparation of the latest expense budget or cash forecast; or an email asking where the extra filters were kept in the coffee room. But no, other than some jokes from friends, no one from my former company had sent anything.

Just then, Gina, my youngest daughter, working at a hotel in Florida, called to tell me she was heading to the beach and wanted to wish me well on my search.

That did wonders for my spirits!

Kyle, my youngest, emailed to let me know that he had successfully arrived in Cincinnati (to begin his final college semester). Since he had flown there two days ago I questioned this latest update. But then I read on and found that, unfortunately, the airline had errantly sent his bags elsewhere. Continuing on, it seems his favorite hat was in one of those bags. And, since the Midwest was experiencing the same miserable weather as we were, in the interest of maintaining his good health he felt it imperative to cut his first few days of classes! (Must remember to check to see if we paid that last tuition bill...)

Ignoring the fact that time was slipping away I reached for my cup of hot coffee and watched the waning snowflakes fall. "Thank God, I don't have to trudge into work this morning," resonated in my mind several times.

As I was about to return to the task at hand, I looked up and there was a vision of *Nanook of the North*. Dressed in a huge red parka, a yellow scarf wrapped around her neck, and a matching ski cap that lacked only the puffy ball to make her look like something from a Peanuts comic strip, there stood the love of my life. Donning woolen mittens, and wearing cute little duck shoes to ward off any dampness from reaching her feet, her outfit would have sufficed for an expedition to Antarctica.

I gently inquired, "WHERE THE HECK ARE YOU GOING?" To which she calmly retorted, "Well, surely not to the beach!

"No," she continued, "I'm on my way out to clear the driveway. One of us has to go to work this morning."

Now, having always walked to the train station, including on mornings such as this, I was unfamiliar with the process of dealing with snowfalls on the home front. I had always assumed that "we" 1) waited for the temperatures to rise above freezing and then let Mother Nature take away that which she had dumped, or 2) had the boys, who have not resided at home in winter for at least three years, shovel it, or 3) paid the kid across the street to clear a path. Confronted with the first storm in my new state of employment, that which is without an income, I voted to go with the first option.

Unfortunately, by the time I was ready to voice my thoughts the love of my life had already left and was hurtling through the garage to undertake the removal of snow from the front of the house!

Could I possibly allow my precious mate to go out there and brave the cold by herself? Yet, I felt it was important for both of us that I actively pursue my next career. Both sides of the issue tore at me.

Chivalry won out. Off I went, in search of appropriate attire to accompany her to what had just recently been christened "the company parking lot."

Fortunately, with the temps so low, the snow was powdery and not at all heavy. Indeed, the biggest problem was to ensure that I was not standing downwind as my partner tossed a load. Having failed to find the correct position twice, I suggested she clean off the cars while I shoveled the driveway. She agreed, and as I continued to scoop Mother Nature's idea of a winter gift, I ruminated on our successful cooperation. It was a good indicator of the potential of our joining forces in her consulting business. (I made a mental note to once again discuss that with her later.)

Two bodies made for quick work.

That is, if more than an hour of shoveling is "quick" work. How readily I have acclimated to working at home!

Upon returning to the warmth of the house, we shared some hot coffee. (Not exactly the Nescafe moment I had once imagined, but life is not a commercial.) Then Elise told me that she would be leaving for the library right after showering.

"Is this your normal routine?" I asked.

"No, it doesn't snow this hard every day!" (Ouch! I must get used to her snappy retorts now that I'm going to be around here a lot more.)

Sensing that I may have been hurt by her sarcasm, she then explained that having taken so

17

much time off over the holidays she had a lot of work awaiting her at a number of clients. And, since she was now the "primary wage earner"...

So, here I now sit at my computer venturing forth into the world provided to me at my desk thanks to the Internet. Of course, bending and lifting were not part of my earlier career activities. As such, my back is aching and my toes are just now getting their feeling back.

Where was I before I was so rudely interrupted by Nanook? Oh yes, I was about to commence the search for the occupation that will fulfill my passion. I must ensure that it will require no physical exertion beyond the tapping of keys on a keyboard.

Speaking of which, if I could only get my fingers to defrost, I could accurately type some of the answers solicited on this first job search site.

Oops, a pop-up just appeared on my screen. It appears that the National Weather Service is forecasting blizzard-like conditions to hit our area this evening. Better not expend all of my energy on the job search today – something tells me "the company parking lot" may need another snow removal tomorrow morning.

Just the thought is taking its toll.

No wait, I think that's my sugar level dropping; perhaps another cup of coffee – but with a donut this time. Wonder if there is still more in the pot?

I will attack the pursuit of my next calling in life later. It is important to be at your peak performance whenever tackling an important project! Ah yes, the lessons learned over a long career in Corporate America will serve me well in the search for my passion, er, I mean, my next career.

Outplacement Center

Whew, it has been a busy month. Semi-retirement, as I have begun to refer to my current employment status, has provided a whole new array of issues in my life. Setting up new daily routines, feverishly addressing my job search (well, maybe not feverishly but with great intentions), and getting used to a new work location, are just a few. Were it not for football I would have a hard time differentiating weekends from weekdays. With the Super Bowl looming I will have to find another way to ensure that I take the proper time to rest each week.

Indeed, this new job status made it difficult to truly enjoy the Martin Luther King holiday a couple of weeks ago. I kept asking "the boss" if it was a formal day off for "our" little company or just another slow Monday. She muttered something about working on the consommé, but my hearing is not so hot, so I just assumed she was ignoring my question. In the interest of maintaining good relations, I stuck with what I believed to be a related thread to her comment and asked what we were having for dinner.

Not that my interest in pursuing the next step of my career is ever far from my consciousness...

Just last week I embarked upon one of my first official excursions from company headquarters

19

(previously known as home) in pursuit of that objective. I ventured off to the Outplacement Center – one of the components of the "offer we could not refuse" made to those being encouraged to leave my former company.

My first take on the term "Outplacement Center" was that it was merely a nice place to stop off on the way to the unemployment office. However, based on my initial thrusts at finding a new calling, I now felt that perhaps I did indeed need some professional guidance. After all, when you have a toothache you go to the dentist, right? And, if an appliance is not working properly, you call a repairman. That is, unless you think it's something you can fix yourself...

Rummaging through the separation materials provided by my former company, I found that which dealt with outplacement. I read, "Outplacement is the structured process of helping unemployed individuals evaluate their career opportunities, implement a job search and manage the transition to new employment..."

Hmm, the bulk of the "incentive package" dealt with exciting me about retirement. This seemed to be a vehicle to entice me to continue working. But if they had wanted me to do so, why had I been encouraged to take the package?

Something smelled fishy.

However, since it was free, how could I not participate? After all, it would only take up some of my time – which lately does not seem to carry very much value. Besides, I miss attending meetings. Breakfasts with the love of my life have not quite fulfilled this need. One morning I even gave her a

PowerPoint presentation on various breakfast options, with the pros and cons of each, but she gave it nary a glance. As such, I called and scheduled myself for one of the upcoming career counseling sessions.

When the big day arrived I donned a sport coat and tie (thank goodness, I had not disposed of all of them). Freshly cologned, I headed out to the address indicated for my first official meeting in months.

Following carefully laid out directions from an Internet map search, I successfully made my way to a small two-story office building in the midst of a trendy little industrial park. The first thing that caught my eye upon entering the building was a directory of the occupants. Upon close examination, I found numerous listings for insurance agents and financial advisors. Was this "counseling" invitation just a scam on their part to get us into their building? Would I get fifteen minutes of career advice and then be shuttled off to other offices to be told how to invest my savings, ensuring that my spouse will live in luxury long after I am gone?

Since I had already made the trip, I found the room number of the Career Placement office and continued on my journey.

Much to my surprise, the outplacement group actually had an entire suite of offices. Being once again in "corporate" mode, I approached the attractive, young receptionist. "Good morning. I am here for a nine A.M. meeting. Could you direct me..." At which point she slowly rose from her desk and, in a clearly bored fashion, showed me the way to a conference room where the seminar was to be held. My meager attempts at small talk fell on deaf ears.

Entering the room, I joined a dozen other similarly aged folks, all with that "deer in the headlights" look. Guess I wasn't the only one to accept the early retirement offer without a plan for the next stage of my life.

After exchanging names, former positions and locations worked, I determined that they were indeed all from my old company. Like me, they also were jaded by years of meetings in similar conference rooms. The difference being that none of us appeared to have anything to *contribute* to this gathering.

The facilitator bounded into the room shortly after the session was scheduled to begin and introduced himself as Bill Humdinger (surely not an assumed name). His energy level was higher than mine and that of my fellow attendees by at least two cups of richly caffeinated coffee. He began his opening remarks with a brief description of his own career to date.

It appears that Bill had also been downsized – he from a marketing job with a large Wall Street investment bank. My guess was that since he got to the Center first, he now has a job and we are on the other side of the table envying his employment status. I made a quick note to check with Bill about employment opportunities at the Outplacement Center, but not until after the other retirees have left.

Taking a page out of *How to Run a Successful Meeting*, Bill asked that we go around the table and introduce ourselves to the group. He suggested we give our name, last position held, and what we hoped to take away from this seminar. This last part had me concerned. I didn't think "the donuts at the coffee table" would be an adequate response.

The first person to speak was a former Group Chief Operator. After giving a brief listing of all past positions held, she wondered how she was going to find a place in the business world that valued knowing how to operate various telephone switchboards. I think she was testing Bill, since the phone company has not used human-operated switchboards for at least thirty years! He quickly assured her that there were numerous companies out there with a need for managers who could handle complex equipment similar to a switchboard. Boy, this guy was good at tap dancing.

Another fellow had been a Network Engineer and expressed a love for boating. He was hoping to find a way to combine his work experience and his passion for the sea. Eying my first opportunity to contribute something, I jumped in with, "You should look into laying underwater telephone cables." It got a small snicker from those familiar with the technology and a blank look from our facilitator. I slumped in my seat with a smug smile on my face.

A former Repair Bureau Manager, looking to be well into Medicare age, explained that having spent over forty years in the business he was not really seeking another career. He had just come to the meeting since he was already bored with staying home in his first months of retirement! I waited for him to say he was also there for the coffee and danish, but he let me down and just sat back in his seat with a dopey grin on his face.

And on it went. Most were like me – lots of experience, no real interest in continuing to do the same, but lacking a "passion" for something else.

Bill complimented all of us on having a good sense of purpose.

Was he listening? Except for the lady who wanted to open a day care center, the rest of us were floundering! He proceeded to insist that there exists a huge demand for experienced, mature managers. I just am not sure that he said where...

He then gave a neat, professionally designed presentation on the wonders of beginning a new career at "mid-life." While I appreciated the compliment, unless medicine makes great strides in the next few years I'm not making plans for using those pension checks collected beyond my hundredth birthday!

Bill proceeded to relate his experience in finding a totally new career in Human Resources after abruptly leaving his last position. Basically, he was laid off when his bank merged with another. He had received the use of this outplacement center as part of his severance package. The fact that they were seeking to hire someone to facilitate seminars such as these was not covered in much depth.

Next, he handed out a workbook that would lead us to a new and exciting livelihood. He assured us it contained several important tools that would enable us to find the perfect employer; which, I assumed, meant one not planning to downsize you within the year following your start date.

After the first hour, I noticed that several of my confreres were doodling on the requisite legal pad which had been left at each seat at the table. Ah yes, experienced, mature managers. I might have guessed they were taking copious notes except for the fact that Bill was just going over the chapter titles in the workbook.

Fortunately, we took a mid-morning break, after which most of us returned to hear the remainder of his pitch. It was obvious that this firm was on retainer, maintaining an arm's length relationship to my former company, since the quality of the donuts was much better than anything I had in the last several years of attending meetings.

Utilizing a massive set of overhead projection slides, Bill walked us through the workbook. Presumably this was important since, though we were all seasoned managers, there may have been some doubt concerning our ability to read. The first chapter had exercises on self-analysis to ascertain our personality traits and the type of work that might suit us best. Great, just what I needed – something to help me determine if I had wasted the last thirty years of my life! That was followed by a section on developing a plan to find the perfect job. Ah yes, the "perfect" plan – I had encountered many of them over the years, each one improving upon the last bit of "perfection."

He then moved into the all-important marketing of ourselves. This was to be done via what was called the "two minute intro," to be used with anyone who may be able to provide a lead on a job. The workbook portrayed it as the golden key to a fruitful job search. It seems that we should have a prepared spiel that encapsulates the reason for our departure from our former employer, our strengths and experience, and our career ambitions – all in a mere ninety seconds! The first thirty seconds are spent getting up the nerve, thus the term "two minute intro." The time parameter stems from what is supposedly the duration of an average elevator ride in an office building, which may be the only time you have with someone who may be the key to opening the door to a successful future career.

Now, I'm not sure where Bill, or the author of the workbook, lives but there are no elevators in our house. Indeed, it takes me less time than that to walk from my office (formerly known as the toy room) to the boss's office (just beyond the kitchen, which often sidetracks my journeys to seek her out). In fact, other than sometimes running into one of the kids or the love of my life, all of whom have already heard my pitch, the only one to talk to is – me! And I find other more interesting things to talk about. So the whole effort in developing the "two minute intro" may be a waste of time.

But I will do it since over thirty years in corporate America teaches you to execute, unquestionably, any direction from someone standing at the head of a conference table with an overhead projector at his beck and call.

Not sure if it was Bill's clearing his throat, but I rallied from my private thoughts and focused again on the man at the front of the room. He was embarking on the importance of creating a comprehensive résumé. This brought a groan from the group, with several commenting that they had never had to prepare one since they worked for the same company their entire lives. He walked us through the basic framework of this important document, leaving it to us to populate it with our individual experiences.

By the time he got to the education section, I had joined my bored confreres in doodling in the margins of the workbook.

Reaching the peak of his perceptivity, Bill recognized the cloud of boredom that had crept silently upon the group and asked us to finish reviewing the workbook at home.

Moving away from the printed matter, he returned to his overhead slides. He presented a display of the vast number of resources available on the Internet. "The Department of Labor has a listing of over seven thousand job titles" (heck, my former company had about the same number). "These might be helpful if you need assistance in identifying the ideal position to which you might aspire."

"Additionally," he continued, "the Small Business Administration has information on starting up your own business." Hmm, wonder if Elise would like me to look into this as a means of revving up "our" little consulting business. It might be the perfect way for me to earn my way into the "company's" executive suite!

As the clock crept toward noon, Bill was running out of gas and had completed his canned presentation. Though nothing he shared was earth shattering, he did instill in us the motivation to go home and work on our résumés.

For some odd reason, at that moment it occurred to me that something my love said to me the other day may have been misunderstood. She had probably said something like, "Work on your résumé," not, "Work on your consommé," which had led me to think she was suggesting I look into a career as a cook!

Rousting myself from my reverie, I heard him conclude the meeting and watched him duck out the door before I could catch his attention. He probably needed to grab lunch before holding an encore performance for another set of unsuspecting retirees in the afternoon. So much for asking about opportunities with the outplacement company...

In two weeks I am scheduled to go to the follow-up seminar. Cannot wait; it may hold the answer to what my next vocation in life is to be. We are to practice our "intros" on live bodies. Wonder if they'll be done in mock elevators?

And so, that is what I was working on earlier today – my two minute intro and my résumé. Can't say that I have made a lot of progress but, more importantly, it is nearly lunchtime and consommé sounds great – wonder if Elise ever did make any?

Business Attire

As I sit here in my new company's headquarters (formerly known as our house) I am perplexed by an issue that I wrestled with at several points in my career. That is, what is considered proper business attire?

Having worked in financial areas for the majority of my career, I wore a suit and tie to work. Sometime in the early eighties came the urge to "loosen up the reins a bit." Those of us who were wearing suits to work were allowed, in some cases even encouraged, to dress more "casually" on Fridays that fell between Memorial Day and Labor Day. It was portrayed as senior management's sensitivity to the desires of the sweating employees beneath them. I suspect that it was done primarily as a cost-saving device – the air conditioning could be turned down early Friday for the duration of the weekend. Of course, that made the "non-casual" Mondays even more dreadful than usual, as it took most of the morning for the AC to get cranked up.

As for me, I was not a big fan of the "casual" decision. Before the change, I never had to worry about stains. It's much harder to cover spilled ketchup or mustard or some of those hot peppers that accompany the gyros from the Greek guy's stand on the corner – you know, the tasty greasy ones that you don't even have to chew, they're so tender, they just slide right down... wait, where was I?

Oh yes, stains – it's difficult to cover a stain on your shirt when you don't have a suit jacket to throw on after lunch. Was I going to have to become a neat-freak just because I was dressed casually?

As for the comfort aspect, well, the heat has never been that big a deal to me. Heck, I wore suits to hot, humid outdoor graduations where even the graduates were wearing shorts beneath their gowns! But nobody consulted me. Once announced, Casual Fridays were a fait accompli.

Then, in the early nineties the trend got worse. Pictures of executives of the booming dot-com companies began appearing in all the business journals. Based in warm and sunny California, they were often attired in jeans and shirts without ties. They were all spreading the new message of success – attained via teamwork and increased productivity gotten through a more relaxed atmosphere. The Eastern business establishment missed the teamwork aspect, focusing instead on the grungy garb as a means of enhancing productivity. Their response was to revise the dress code policy to incorporate casual dress on all Fridays throughout the year! Sweaters without worn out elbows became a new concern of mine.

In the late nineties, prior to the bursting of the dot-com bubble, a further attempt to emulate the ongoing success of the left-coast contingent was made. Still hoping to capture some of the Silicon Valley charisma, dress policies were once again revised; "business casual" attire was mandated for all days of the week! Note the insertion of the word "business" into what had previously been just plain "casual." This was still Manhattan, not Silicon Valley; perhaps that was behind the appended adjective.

Since those in Human Resources, who wrote the policy, never did fully explain what was meant by the phrase, "business casual," I witnessed the full gamut of interpretations. Men's attire ranged from dress pants and shirt without a tie, to jeans with a golf shirt, to even worse. There was a guy in IT who came in dressed in torn jeans, tie-dye T-shirt, and, I am serious here, rope sandals! I was tempted to cry out, "Get a job, Hippie!" only to remember that he was the guy who rescued me every time my monitor displayed the blue screen of death.

After several years of contending with business casual, I took a position on the staff of the VP of Finance. Alas, the curtain in front of the wizard was removed. All those on the executive floors wore the classic white shirt and tie. Away went the sport shirts and slacks. I resumed wearing a suit until my last day with the company.

Which brings us to the matter at hand – how should I now dress as I gear up for work at my new office (formerly known as the toy room)?

Not one to act rashly, I did some research and have come across several differing opinions on this subject. Some have suggested that an advantage of working at home is that you can extend your work day by rolling out of bed and working in your pajamas! Obviously, they have not seen me "roll" out of bed. Stagger, maybe, but roll? I don't think so. And, as for pajamas, do boxers qualify? How do they suggest you explain such dress when answering the door for the FedEx gal making a delivery?! Might this be a bit too "casual"?

Other literature on the subject conveys that one should dress for the type of work one is seeking.

Since I am looking to possibly reenter the business world as a professional, I assume I should dress as one. But based on my prior experience, that still leaves the question of "business or business casual attire?" If the former, must I once again pull out my ties? And if the latter, do I dare go as far as my friend in IT? I'm not sure I even own a pair of rope sandals.

Wanting to maintain some degree of decorum, I have elected to continue the discipline of a traditional shower and shave each morning, followed up by a generous dousing of cologne – hey, have you seen the FedEx gal? I then envision myself going downstairs to the office, with a coffee and donut in hand, since that makes it seem a bit more official, but wait...

I am still not sure what I should be wearing in the office.

Long have I subscribed to the management tenet that directs one who is confronted with a problem to put all of the issues down on paper. Doing so enables one to calmly examine each aspect of the conundrum, as well as potential options and strategies, subsequently arriving at a good solution. Perhaps a review of my personal dress classifications will facilitate a decision.

Growing up in a small, first-generation Italian enclave I learned to compartmentalize clothing. Yes, under the careful tutelage of my mother I learned that each piece of clothing fits into one of three categories.

At the top were "Sunday," or "dress," clothes. While this label may be familiar to many (you know, "dress shirts," "dress pants," and so on), in the vernacular of my early home, this also encompassed all items not yet worn. Clothing newly purchased or received as gifts could not be worn without first wearing them to church – it ensured some sort of blessing upon them. (I don't remember any such assurance in the Baltimore Catechism but my mother insisted it was the gospel truth.) This category, which subsequently evolved to "business attire," became what I wore to work in the early years of my career.

Since I don't feel the need to embrace this style of dress in my current position, that is, unless I have clients visiting for the day (pardon the wishful thinking), I am leaning toward a bit more casual style.

Might that be the category of what Mom called "everyday" clothes? A far cry from the first category, these were presentable, if not fashionable, yet always neat and clean. They were the outfits donned for school, that is, before entering the parochial high school with its mandated uniform. Indeed, if the material could still hold a crease, it would have one. Oh, those warm, nurturing days when the iron was out as often as the cereal bowls – I still remember putting on dungarees with a sharply defined crease!

After leaving the old homestead, "everyday" clothes took on a more mature meaning. Jeans gave way to khakis which with a golf, or sport shirt became the outfit of choice; unless there was manual labor to be done. Indeed, along with a sport coat, this came to be my answer for what comprised "business casual" attire. But is this really necessary as I sit alone at my computer doing whatever it is that this "company" requires of me or in the pursuit of the next step in my career? Should I take "business casual" down to another level completely?

That last classification is what was known, while growing up, as "play" clothes. Ah yes, once the "everyday" stuff got stained, torn beyond Mom's miraculous mending ability, or had irreparably broken zippers they became "play" clothes. (Speaking of broken zippers, ever wonder why kids find it so easy to play doctor?) Adding to these were the clothes that were the victim of the infamous growth spurts that elevated cuffs to more than three inches above your shoes or wrists. The bottom line was that these were clothes with which you could do anything; that is, short of leaving them at a friend's house, which would incur the rarely seen, but nevertheless feared, wrath of Mom Della Rocca.

More recently, as I began playing less and working around the house more, I have come to call these "work" clothes. Again, you may be familiar. The old college sweatshirt with the cutoff sleeves and frayed collar, coupled with the worn Levi's that have mustard and beer stains gotten at that final playoff game at the stadium. Are these acceptable garb to wear while seeking future professional employment? Will such an outfit color the database program that I am developing for one of Elise's clients? Will I tend to use slang instead of proper language in some of the forms? Instead of "Street, City, State, and Zip Code" might I put, "Where do you live?"

And you probably thought this whole issue was a stupid one!

Well, so much for listing all of my options as a means of answering the question of how to dress

34

during my time of career transition. I am still not sure where I stand on the subject. Perhaps I just need to print out all of my choices.

Of course, I could easily do so if I hadn't just spilled coffee on the printer and cannot seem to get it to work! Oh boy, now where is that guy with the sandals? The current technical support staff is the love of my life. Oh boy, that will not be a happy meeting.

Probably won't bring up the dress code issue with her. Maybe I will just take a poll of employee preferences.

But no, that won't do – I still don't know how I would vote, and I'm fifty percent of the staff...

So much for resolving the dress code issue. Guess I'll just get something to eat in the company cafeteria (formerly known as the kitchen); it's always easier to think on a full stomach. Perhaps I should first put on a pair of pants.

Now, which to wear?

New Beginnings

And so begins another wonderful day. I have to tell you, many of those concerns about early retirement are quickly disappearing. I am beginning to like sleeping in and having a leisurely breakfast with my bride, though the latter are fewer than I would like to believe. But wait, before I make it seem too appealing, let me bring you up to date on my continuing pursuit of the perfect next career.

As you may recall, a few weeks ago our hero (yours truly) was attending an Outplacement Workshop – being led by someone who had very recently been "surplused" himself.

Well, yesterday I attended the second day of the aforementioned workshop. Arriving several minutes before it was scheduled to begin; I recognized some of the same faces from the previous session. The room seemed much larger than I had recalled. Indeed, shortly after the arrival of our peppy facilitator, I realized why. My impression of the cavernous appearance of the room was a result of the fact that there was a significant drop in the number of attendees.

Reinforcing a comfort level that none of us felt, he once again introduced himself as Bill Humdinger. (Could that really be his name? Might he just be using it to keep us from looking him up after the session ends? It's not like he's all that talented.)

Bill must be pretty sharp, as he had arrived at the same impression I had noted, and made note of the smaller group. Reestablishing his never-ending optimism, he insisted that the reduction would be beneficial to completing the tasks that he had planned for the day. (Again, he showed his tap dancing ability.)

Not hesitant to jump right in, he began by asking each of us to describe our endeavors in seeking employment or preparing ourselves for the next step in our careers.

Oblivious to the first few responses, offered only after a lot of prodding by Bill, I instead focused on what I would say. Surely, he would not want to hear about my setting up an office in what was formerly our toy room. Might I tell him of the discussions I have had with "the boss" (I might delay mentioning she is also my wife) about becoming a partner in her little consulting business? Though, in reality, those conversations have been shorter than the time I might be asked to speak this morning.

Fortunately, one of the members of the group had been very ambitious and was quite verbose in sharing his experience with the group. Patrick had attended several interviews, resulting from the mailing of his résumé to a number of firms prior to our initial meeting. (He was a bit younger than most of us and, as I recall, had been with a few companies prior to joining my former employer.) Though his results were far from encouraging, everyone peppered him with all kinds of questions.

My guess was that no one was actually interested in what he had to say; rather they were merely stalling in hopes they would not be asked to explain what they'd been doing. After almost a half-hour of critiquing the poor guy's performance to date, Bill asked if anyone else had done anything constructive since our last meeting.

Though tempted to relate my wrestling with the business attire issue, I passed. Not one to monopolize a meeting, I sat quietly – as did all of my colleagues.

When no one volunteered, Bill suggested we move along since we only had the room for the morning. Smiles of success in our delay tactics appeared around the table.

Pulling out another massive set of overheads, he commenced addressing the key to a successful job search – networking. Essentially, the concept is that each time you speak to someone about your career you should ask them for the names of at least three others with whom you might speak on the same subject. The presumption being that if you do this enough times, and with sufficient frequency (roughly twice each day), you will make contact with every citizen in the State of New York within the next six months. This last estimate was done by me, in the margins of the workbook, while Bill was doing his presentation, so don't hold me to the accuracy therein.

Bill then pulled a small notebook from his jacket pocket. (Did I mention that he was wearing a suit at each of our meetings? Ah, the sweet smell of success.) He proudly displayed the little leatherbound note pad, telling us, "I always carry this with me. In it I have the names and phone numbers of all those with whom I have networked while finding this latest position.

"I keep each contact in my personal business community informed of my current career step," he proudly continued, "and ask them if there is any way that I may be of service. These are important aspects of networking – to keep it fresh and mutually beneficial." As for me, it sounded like Bill was not too confident that this gig was going to last, and he was preparing to be back on our side of the table. But, hey, what do I know? I was a finance guy, not human resources professional. How would I know how precarious outplacement work is?

Bill explained that he had often made use of his brief introductory statement (aka "two minute intro") and would now like to hear how we had progressed in developing ours. We were to do this by standing and pairing up with a neighboring conferee. As subsequently directed, we rolled out our "two minute intros" on each other, and then moved on to repeat the process with our next neighbor. By the fourth one, I was emulating pushing a button on an elevator and getting vertigo from the numerous simulations of going up and down!

If I heard one more person telling me who they were and why they were no longer with my old company, I would spit. I knew why they were here – they all received the same "offer they could not refuse," and left because it was better than staying.

What was of mild interest was to hear how some of them put different spins on the dilemma. Indeed, in some cases, they felt the alternative had too much downside and were quick to express as much in a series of moans and groans. "The bums at my former company were about to demote all managers over the age of fifty." "They were going to force all of us to work four day work weeks, with a commensurate drop in pay." And then there was the best of all, "Rumor had it that the company was to be sold and they were going to bring in an entirely new management team." (My former company's management team numbered in excess of seventy thousand.) Not sure, but I really don't think those folks were going to enhance their chances of finding fruitful contacts.

Fun people like that are the reasons I push to the rear of an elevator. I keep my eyes locked on the little lights flashing the floor numbers, avoiding any conversation at all. Forget about the "two minute intro!"

After we had rehearsed to a point that we were all comfortable with our spiels, our leader tossed us a curve ball. "Perhaps a thirty-second intro might be more appropriate."

He must have sensed that the others had the same lack of access to an elevator in their homes. "Since your new target audience may no longer be the chieftains of industry you might bump into within the skyscrapers of New York, it is important to practice for other encounters. Like the mail woman, UPS deliveryman," (and the short, fat guy taking our order at the deli, I mentally contributed), "in the event that they might have suggestions on how to jump-start your careers." (Wonder how I would look in a mayo- and mustard-stained apron?)

After numerous false starts, Bill recognized that such ad hoc revisions to our lengthier intros were not going to be readily achieved by this group. "Just work on it at home. But don't delay; you may have need for it sooner than you think." (Could he possibly know how often I go to the deli?)

With that admonition, Bill took note of the fact that the noon hour was approaching, and with it our formal outplacement counseling was to come to an end. After some brief closing remarks, he wished us well in our future endeavors and packed up his briefcase.

In retrospect, the session had been much more than just preparing personal sales pitches. We learned of the myriad opportunities for, as Bill described so well, "former managers and midlevel executives, now in their fifties, with a wealth of experience and knowledge gained over careers of thirty-plus years in a very well-respected company." This guy had really done his homework about who was paying his company's fee.

Indeed, between the formal presentations and the brief individual conversation I had had with my new "mentor" during the morning break, I gained confidence that there might indeed be a successful career path ahead of me. Bill was supportive of my dreams of the possibilities of short work weeks, at lucrative pay, and plenty of vacation time. Though, from the remarks in the room, there would be a lot of competition. And no, he never did offer me his phone number. Nevertheless, I left popping buttons with my newly found confidence (as well as a few donuts that were left over from the break).

I'm now sitting here waiting for the doorbell to ring. I've got my thirty second bit down pat. And, if whoever is there happens to have some time, I will gladly roll out my two minute intro. Hey, it might be the Regional FedEx Director subbing in for the usual gal. You never know, it may lead to something fruitful.

The Return

The job search was placed on hold for some unexpected consulting work last week. I was taking a plunge back into the Corporate America.

It started with a phone call on Monday. The voice on the other end was that of someone from my past. My last boss, Cliff Engelmann, was calling.

Cliff opened with the usual queries about how retirement was treating me. (He never did grasp the idea that I did not view my departure as "retirement.") In reply, I briefly related my relentless search for the next step of my career. He chided me for not just enjoying the good life. (Easy for him to say, he is still on the short side of fifty and thinks of "early retirement" as just an extended vacation involving hammocks and margaritas.)

Just as I was thinking this might be nothing more than a call to renew a friendship, he dropped the tone of his voice to that which I had become accustomed to hearing when there was some unpleasant task to be done. "I was wondering if you might be interested in doing some consulting work.

"Do you recall that COVIS program that you developed a few years ago? I thought I understood how it worked, but have come up a bit short. And since our submission is due by the end of the month..."

He then spent the next few minutes stroking my ego before relating that no one of my colleagues left behind was able to grasp the program that was done but once each year. "Though the documentation you created prior to leaving was exceptional," the flattery, though welcome, was so out of character that I had to withhold a laugh, "this particular process has proven to be too much for the guys." At this point, I fully expected that he was going to try to lure me out of retirement! Might this be the unanticipated answer to my quest?

No; he was merely seeking my help for a few days to develop some written instructions, after which I might come in for a day, or so, to run the program and train some new people. I knew he was desperate when he offered to pay me a princely sum for my labors. (Well, maybe not princely, but hey, compared to my current income anything looks appealing.) If I had known such a failure to leave behind comprehensive procedures would lead to a lucrative consulting job, I might have been a bit less diligent about others I had done. I agreed to do what I could.

The next few hours found me clearing the cobwebs from the business side of my mind; mentally reconstructing the program to which Cliff had alluded. Not having taken any of the related paperwork or files, I had to work totally from memory. Oh boy, that's not one of my stronger attributes – I have a hard time recalling what we had for dinner last evening.

And so it was that I donned my old corporate hat for the next few days. Fortunately, those processes that had been my bread and butter for so long came back as readily as the recollection of the tastiness of those donuts from Mahmud's coffee truck. I was pleased to see I could still build a relatively clear set of instructions even without the aforementioned work material.

The last step would be to venture into the Big Apple to share my results with those who would be carrying them forward, two young women who had joined the department since my departure.

A wind chill of near-zero on that Friday morning had my face frozen halfway to the station, reminding me of how right it was to have taken the separation package when offered. Once I arrived in the city, I opted to take the subway for the short distance to my building. I had always walked in the past, but the train had arrived a bit late and I did not want to further reduce the time I had to complete my instructions and convey them to the new team. Nor did I want to have to make this a multiple-day effort; I had the search for my new career to pursue.

Now, the subway is a means of commuting that I had avoided for most of my career in New York. The cars are always crowded and rarely comfortable. I've heard that they've been cleaned up and made quieter over the years. But the clientele has not changed much and that was always ninety percent of the whole underground commute problem.

Not having ridden them in several years, I was first surprised to see that they no longer used those little metal tokens. Of course, they had not converted to using good old U.S. currency. No, now you have to go to an ATM-like machine and purchase a plastic card which allows you to move through the turnstiles.

Ah, those turnstiles. They use the ones with those metal bars that are always a threat to your manhood if you happen to try to push through before the system was good and ready to allow you entry! I slowed my rapid pace to ensure that all lights were green, providing an easily swinging gate for my entrance.

Having successfully negotiated my way onto the platform, I found myself in the midst of a mob of people, all waiting to board the next train. It was bad enough that there were so many people, but in addition, most were carrying BACKPACKS!

This latest means of carrying books, newspapers, lunches, and God knows what else are going to lead to the ruination of this great country we call America! Excuse me for living, but I just lost ten pounds, thanks to the South Beach Diet, and am now carrying a pretty svelte two hundred pounds on my six foot one inch frame. So why isn't there any room for me on the subway? Backpacks!

The tiniest person in America is now at least two feet wider then ever before. And do they ever think of taking the darn thing off their back while forcing their way onto a car that's already too crowded because there are fifty other backpack-toting losers already in the car? Noo!! You have to find a way to squeeze your significantly reduced personal frame (did I mention I lost ten pounds due to the South Beach Diet?) in between two heavily inflated backpacks which are squeezing out the little bit of air still left in your lungs.

Then, upon reaching their stop, they don't apologize as they walk over your asphyxiated, limp (but much leaner) body because they don't know they just killed you. And the reason they don't know that is because they can't feel anything through their backpacks... I mean how could you when you're at least two canvas covered feet away from your latest victim?!

Now, I'm not one to complain, but I miss the days when the subway was ruled by real men who carried hard-shelled briefcases, never put them down, and smacked your kneecap every time the subway car screeched to an unscheduled halt. Yeah, those were the days when a subway ride was a subway ride, and a broken kneecap was a badge of honor.

But I digress... Where was I?

Ah yes, having exited the subway I made the last short jaunt to my old stomping ground. Anticipating a hot cup of Java and a donut, I was disappointed to find that Mahmud was nowhere to be seen. Had he relocated to a more lucrative corner in Manhattan? Might so many of his former customers "taken the package" that he no longer had sufficient clients to warrant staying? Plowing on, I made my way in to the massive lobby hoping that the coffee room was still being productively used.

It did not take me long to find that, though a retiree, I was now persona non-gratis at the company to which I had dedicated over thirty of the best years of my life. A company ID, such as that forfeited several months ago, was required to gain entrance to the building's offices. Though the guards may have recognized me, they followed instructions in a way that would make most managers envious. "No ID, no entry."

Hmm, first the bitter cold commute, then the battle of the subway, then the failure to grab a cup of warming java, and now this. It was not shaping up to be a momentous return to Corporate America.

While stewing about my predicament, an old acquaintance, whose name escaped me, saw me and stopped. "Hi! It's been a while since I've seen you. Where do they have you working now?"

I explained that I had not been transferred to another office but had "taken the package," making it sound like a prescription medicine. "My old boss called and asked me to come in to do some training, but I can't seem to get by the 'rent-a-cop' without an ID. My driver's license doesn't seem to cut it."

Being pretty perceptive, and also probably anxious to get on with her day, she offered to vouch for me and sign me in as a visitor. Having done so, and possibly fearing that I would next ask her for money to get a coffee, she quickly bade me farewell and headed to her elevator. The finance offices being near the top of the building, I boarded one heading there.

The familiar scents of the building brought back fond memories. However, boarding an elevator for the first time in months was a disappointment as there was no one with whom I could share my "two minute intro."

As I stepped onto my old floor I was surprised at the number of new faces. Two turns and I soon found some former colleagues who had elected to stay or, more likely, had insufficient time in the business to even consider leaving. Hands were shaken and smiles exchanged. The conversations with friends were too short and those with mere acquaintances too long. In neither case did it seem appropriate to subject them to my "two minute intro." Continuing on, I hastened to find Cliff and the opportunity to meet the new kids on the block.

He was gracious in welcoming me back, but I found that some things never change. Not five minutes into our meeting, he explained that he had to rush off to another meeting. Exiting his office, he did first lead me to an office where I could access the departmental data I needed to enable him to meet his requirements by Monday. I took this as confirmation that my consulting gig was indeed not to extend beyond today.

Though it felt strange to walk the floors after exactly two months, three weeks, and five days, I immediately fell back into that comfort zone of doing a job that I had mastered over the years.

Sitting at the computer and retrieving some old files, I found that I had recalled even more than I expected. Using the data therein, I quickly populated the program. I then modified the procedures that I had created at home to better reflect the procedure. It was not long before I had completed that which would enable the "rookies" to function. Ah, the sweet feelings of success and experience were enervating. During the afternoon, I would sit with the neophytes and go over the program, answering any questions they might have.

Joining a few old buddies for lunch broke up what would become a rather taxing day. Mike was still moaning about the state of the company and the economy in general. Joe was in the midst of still another divorce. And Harry was happy as ever about the fact that his team had won another Super Bowl. Jokes were exchanged, rumors shared, and an update of who else had taken the package rounded out the conversation. Ah, the same old shop talk. It felt like putting on a favorite old pair of shoes.

The afternoon found me sitting in a conference room with two lovely young ladies. Olivia, raven-haired and a certified accountant had only been with the company for a year. Madison, blonde and a bit of a ditz, had worked for the company for seven years, and was hoping to find a rich husband soon so she could quit and live on his income. Their perfumes permeated the air.

Reminding myself that I did not want to get caught in the weekend rush hour commute, I refocused their attention on the matter at hand. Spending considerable time on the fine nuances of the COVIS program and its importance to the functioning of the company (my assessment, not so sure that Cliff felt the same way). I then went over that which I had done in the morning which was sufficient to meet the commitment for this round of submissions. They seemed most pleased with that last bit of information.

Turning to the computer in the room, I then worked my way through the procedures I had prepared. It seemed to hold the attention of at least one of them, as the other seemed to be busy doing a lot of texting on her smartphone. I wasn't sure if Madison was keying copious notes or making plans for the weekend.

Before I knew it, the time was approaching the cocktail hour. As intellectually strenuous as it had been, I was pleased with the apparent success of my training. They seemed to fully grasp what I had shown them. Either I was very good or these two gals were very sharp. I elected to believe the former.

Bidding my new friends farewell, I headed down the hall to say so long to Cliff and my former colleagues. However, they must have introduced some new departure time for Fridays since they were all gone.

Donning my coat I climbed into the familiar elevator one more time. Funny, but the whole time I rode, no one else came on. Thus passed my last opportunity to use my "two minute intro!"

Buoyed by a sense of accomplishment from a job well done, I elected to walk to the train station, thus avoiding the infamous subway. Of course, I subsequently found myself standing the whole way home on a weather-delayed commuter train. The ride only confirmed my decision to seek a new career that would not require the use of any type of mass transit.

And so begins a new week. I am intent on finding the "right" livelihood, with an opportunity to work close to home. And who better to know about such opportunities than those who make a living in the area. Forget the "two minute and thirty second intros;" I have a platter of cookies and brownies awaiting the Postwoman, UPS delivery guy, or Jehovah's Witness – whoever arrives at the front door first. I figure that after they have indulged a bit, they might be more willing to provide those precious contacts that may lead to a new career!

Man with a Sash

At last, a warm day to rid us of some of the snow! The sun is shining and the temperatures are very spring-like, expected to reach into the low fifties today. It seems hard to believe that just over a week ago I was in Manhattan for the Saint Patrick's Day Parade.

My son, Adam, in the capacity of tour guide, was meeting up with a high school marching band from northern Alabama. They were to participate in the world-famous parade. He needed an assistant and asked if I was interested in fulfilling that role. Little did I know at the time that it might lead to a potentially fulfilling new calling in life.

The morning dawned cloudy and quite chilly, though the first day of spring was a mere four days away. Cold and windy was the forecast. Temperatures would sneak into the low forties, but the wind chill factor would make it feel closer to freezing. I dressed in layers to ensure that I could successfully weather the upcoming day.

Throughout my career, Long Island Railroad commutes on St. Patrick's Day were always the worst. Oh, there were other bad days, due to storms and equipment breakdowns, but they were all unexpected. This was the one day you knew was going to be a disaster both going in and returning home at night.

51

Trips on the LIRR were not the comfortable rides portrayed in movies set in the suburbs of a major city. Rather than the nattily dressed actors and extras, these trains were usually crowded with bleary-eyed, sleep-deprived, harried business people. If you were fortunate to get on at an early station you could avoid being one of the ten or fifteen in each car that ended up standing for the fifty to sixty minute ride. Most rode with their heads buried in the morning's newspapers. Some were even venturous enough to bring along a cup of coffee to drink while being jostled along the tracks of steel.

On a typical St. Patty's Day, the normal crowd would be supplemented by what seemed like half of Long Island's high school and college student population. All garbed in varying shades of green and pumped up for a day of unsupervised debauchery! Instead of the fellow dozing off next to me in my customary seat, on this day I often had to fight to find a seat at all. And then, it would often be next to a garishly dressed youngster trying hard not to spill her oversized *Slurpee* or *Venti Caramel Macchiato*. If lucky, the only stains I would carry off to work would be those on my fingers from the cheaply produced newspaper.

It was with such memories that I awaited the train that most recent holiday morning. Standing on the platform I scanned an emerald sea. The "regular" commuters looked younger than I remembered. Many of them were wearing scarves or sweaters of green. But the bulk of the color was from the youth movement that was there en masse. Green sweatshirts, pants, hats, and even some presumably recently dyed hair foreshadowed the day to come.

Their energy contrasted sharply on that Friday morning against that of the "regulars" whose only joy was that it was TGIF day. And even that was tempered by the chill wind blowing across the unprotected elevated platform.

My seating skills, honed over a great many years, had not diminished. I hip checked a young man two rows down the train aisle, enabling me to slide into one of the few remaining seats. I then found myself next to a petite young woman wearing a sweatshirt that proclaimed her as being Irish, though I sensed from her straight, jet black hair and eyes that she was Asian. Throughout the ride, she conversed with her friends who were sitting across the aisle and two rows forward. I gleaned that they were college students. One of the guys in the row ahead had the group's communal flask which was providing their "warm-up" before the parade. Ah yes, some things never change.

I was to meet Adam and the rest of the group at the corner of 44th Street and Sixth Avenue by nine. I arrived a full half-hour early. As the wind was whipping down the streets which intersect the broad avenues, I regretted not wearing a hat as Elise had suggested. Earmuffs and a scarf, accoutrements of commutes that were now a memory, remained forgotten in the closet – oh, how I wished I had them then.

With such thoughts running through my mind, my eyes came to rest on one of the many street vendors who had set up for the day. They were selling all kinds of St. Patrick's paraphernalia, from buttons displaying *Kiss Me I'm Irish* to "genuine" Irish shillelaghs. I had to laugh, since these same vendors sell hot dogs and pretzels every other day of the year!

Sauntering over in hopes of finding something to wear on my head, my eyes settled on a knit green hat bedecked with a large white pom-pom and emblazoned with *Erin Go Bragh*. Tempted to ask for a translation, I passed since the Latino vendor was surely no more familiar with Gaelic than me! Though not normally a hat person, the electric feel of the day, coupled with the cold and, most importantly, a price tag of only a sawbuck convinced me that I could survive wearing it for the next several hours. Pulling it on, I felt like I had become Tam O'Shanter himself!

The buses with Adam and his charges pulled up shortly after nine. They disembarked quickly. After laughing heartily at my purchase, Adam quickly transitioned into professional mode. He explained that he was to take the chaperones uptown where they would view the parade near its terminus. I was to stay with the band until they joined the parade and then grab a cab to meet him. Being a native New Yorker, I would be the liaison between Dwight, the Band Director, and the parade officials.

Bidding Adam farewell, I sauntered over to introduce myself to Dwight. A slow talking Southerner, he told me that he had gone to some "big time" music school in Jackson, Mississippi. This was his first visit to the Big Apple and, like many on the trip, he was in awe of the size and speed of the city – picture Forrest Gump meets Wall Street.

Dwight handed me a package of instructions which had been sent to him by the parade organizers. It detailed their placement within the cavalcade of formally dressed police, high school bands, Hibernian society members, and various other ethnic groups. Our group was to merge into the parade, which began two blocks south on Fifth Avenue, when directed to do so by parade officials. We would be the first of twenty-six high school bands in the parade that was to eventually have a hundred and sixty thousand participants!

The kids were well-disciplined. Hustling off the buses, they gathered halfway down the blockaded street to get into formation. Dressed in their fancy uniforms, including plumed hats, they looked like every other marching band I had seen in Thanksgiving and New Year's Day Parades over the years. Then my eyes caught a glimpse of the baton twirlers. They were in bright red warm-up suits. I wondered if the flimsy outfits would keep them warm on this rather blustery morning. Dwight, not wanting his charges to worry about the cold, distracted them by taking them through their musical scales and warm-up exercises.

The parade was to begin at ten o'clock, with our group joining in about fifteen minutes later. Believing we had everything in hand I took note of an important-looking man – he wore a colorful sash over his caramel-colored top coat, approaching Dwight. Fearing that the latter would not understand anyone without a deep Southern accent, I remembered my role as liaison and quickly jumped into action.

"Can I help you?"

"Yes, are you responsible for the Buford High School Band?"

Hesitant to usurp the Band Director's authority, yet with a head swelling with assumed responsibility, I answered in my best Southern drawl, "Why, yes siree, I am!"

In reply, he thrust his hand into a bag he was carrying and tossed me an impressive looking gold sash. "Here, wear this. Other members of the parade committee will be looking for you. They will give you further instructions." And he was off.

Unfurling the sash, I saw that it was emblazoned with *PARADE COMMITTEE.* Wow, between this and the fuzzy hat atop my head I was really getting into the exhilaration of the day. Until this point, it was just another raucous St. Patty's Day in New York.

With my new sense of importance, I traversed up and down the street as the band and dancers continued their preparations. My chest bulged beneath the newly donned sash. But then I noticed that, what seemed like, every other person on the block was wearing some sort of sash as well! I wondered if my little Latino friend who had sold me the hat also sold parade sashes.

At last, some time on the far side of ten, I could see the parade had begun, led by hundreds of uniformed police officers marching up Fifth Avenue. And, just at that time, our school's dancers began to disrobe. They dropped their warm-up pants and shucked their jackets, leaving long stocking legs that did not quit and bare arms sticking out of sleeveless torso-covering glittered tops! Some of the chaperones had hung back with us and they proceeded to stuff the outer garments into large plastic bags, after which they headed for cabs to meet their friends uptown. I shuddered from the cold, or was that from looking at the two southern belles leading the troupe?! These were high school kids? Wow!

As my mind reeled, one of the many sash-wearing officials approached me and asked if I was with the Buford Band. I answered in the affirmative – I was being very formal. With reddened cheeks and appearing to be on the verge of a coronary, he screamed that we belonged on the east, not west, side of Fifth Avenue – and on 46th, not 44th, Street!! Oh boy, a parade official for less than an hour and already I had screwed up! How could it be?

Not wanting to lose face, I pulled out the paperwork Dwight had given me. Once I confirmed that we were indeed in the right place, I shared it with the official. But, no, Mr. Cardiac Arrest had a whole binder of similar sheets, and he pointed to their time stamp of six that morning. I looked at mine and it was dated March 15 – a full two days earlier. "Must be your first time. Not to worry, it's important to stay flexible at these parades. Now get this group moved!"

Approaching Dwight to tell him of this latest change of events, I wondered how difficult it would be to reposition the band. The two blocks north would be relatively easy, we could work our way up the parallel Sixth Avenue. But then, how on earth would we ever get the hundred and fifty band members across Fifth Avenue which was now flooded with the blue coats of New York's finest?! Oh boy, where was Adam?

While explaining this predicament to the Director, I noticed that the rear of the band was "leaking" toward Sixth Avenue! Still another official had obviously usurped our control and was leading the group, Pied Piper fashion, to their new gathering point, or so I hoped. We immediately fell in behind them, trotting up the street.

As I had experienced in prior years, 46th Street was like all the other streets – filled with revelers, all trying to see some of the parade before heading for the nearest open bar. It turned out that our Pied Piper was actually a similarly-sashed parade coordinator, accompanied by two burly members of New York's Mounted Police Force. Our group made it to 46th Street and the barriers blocking the crowds from flowing onto Fifth, where we awaited a break in the action to cross. Sure enough, within minutes, there was a pause in the parade and we were directed to bolt across the avenue – no disciplined marching here!

Regrouping on the other side, we were met by even more official looking sashes. But these were not just gold – they had various stripes of green and Irish emblems. I sensed that the more regalia on the sash, the more important the official. Recognizing me as one of "them," I was told we had fifteen minutes to line up before being called in to the parade. I conveyed as much to the Director, who was taking all of this excitement surprisingly well. I was a basket case!

The parade continued to stream before us when Dwight and the head Baton twirler, a tall lithesome southern belle, hit me with a question of protocol. "Someone with a sash told Melanie that as the band arrives at the reviewing stand at St. Patrick's Cathedral they were to stop and she, as the Baton Leader, was to climb the steps and reverentially kiss the Cardinal! Is this, indeed, the tradition?"

I did not have the heart to tell them that I had never gotten even this close to the parade route, let alone the reviewing stand. However, maintaining my professional demeanor, I told him I would get an answer.

Breaking through the barriers, trying to look like I was on official business so as not to be stopped by one of the many cops monitoring the crowds, I sought out one of the officials who had first greeted us on our arrival on this side of the avenue. Getting his attention, I broached the question of protocol. Laughing heartily, he explained with a deep Irish brogue, "No, you are not to stop anywhere along the parade route unless directed to do so by one of the many officials along the route. And, NO ONE IS TO APPROACH THE REVIEWING STAND!"

I returned to reassure the lovely young Baton Majorette, that there was no need to stop. She nearly hugged me she was so relieved. "I didn't mind the kissing part, that didn't bother me. But, being Southern Baptist, I have no idea who the Cardinal is!"

About half past ten we finally got our directive to "march into the parade." I was impressed to see how smoothly the band responded to Dwight's subsequent order. Unrehearsed, they blended in and within a block appeared as though they had been with the parade from the start. Thus began a four mile trek in front of what was later reported to be in excess of two million onlookers.

Though I was supposed to catch a cab uptown to meet Adam, I got swept up in the surge and found myself marching along with the drummers! My golden sash gave me a look of belonging, which was important since I had neither the band's uniform nor the shapely legs of the baton twirlers! For the next two hours I walked along, smiling, wondering if anyone noticed the guy who looked like a leftover from the Columbus Day Parade.

As I marched, I forgot that I was still wearing the tacky knit cap labeled *Erin Go Bragh*. Not sure if it was the hat, but I must have had half the onlookers shout that phrase to me throughout the duration of the parade. In retrospect, I wish it had said *Kiss Me I'm Irish* since there were some truly lovely lasses lining the parade route!

We passed the reviewing stand without any incidents, though I think I saw Melanie looking to see if she could figure which one was the Cardinal. I later explained that he was the only guy with a head piece taller than her band's Drum Major!

Then, not two blocks after the Cathedral some guy pulled me to the side and asked if I was with the band. Noting that he had numerous badges and ribbons on his sash, I answered positively, expecting to get some new instructions. Instead, over a breath that smelled like what I assumed was Irish whiskey, he regaled me with his opinion that the "marching gals" were the best he had seen in years of watching the parade. He wanted to "give them a little something," at which point he handed me two crisp hundred dollar bills! After effusively thanking him, I trotted to the head of the group to tell the Director about the largesse just handed to me. Only in New York!

The march terminated just above 86th Street and the kids had no interest in staying to watch the rest of the parade. They just wanted to get onto the warm buses which were awaiting them. Their next clearly expressed desire, shouted through the windows, was to get something to eat!

Dwight, beaming with a glow that accompanies the attainment of a hard-earned objective, gathered the baton twirlers together before they got onto their bus. I overheard one girl say that they expected to get some grief about having dropped a baton or two! Instead, he spoke to them quietly, and then it became evident he had told them of the "gift" – they let out a yell that had the rest of the band staring at them through the bus windows.

Adam, having found me, asked where I had been. He had been expecting me to join him much earlier and was shocked to see me walking along the avenue with the band. I explained that as a parade official – I held out my sash – I was merely fulfilling what I assumed to be my duty. I told him I was thinking of joining the following year's St. Patrick's Day Parade Committee.

Unfortunately, I have since found that they require some Irish heritage.

Oh well, there is always the Thanksgiving Day Parade. At most, they may require that one has been called a turkey at least once in their life. And if so, I will clearly qualify. Hey, this parade gig was fun. I have never had so many people cheer for me while performing my duties.

Or were they cheering for the long legged young gals marching alongside me?

I will continue to think they were cheering for the man with the sash!

This whole parade thing could open up a new career path for me!

Wood Finisher

"Crisis! Vandals have struck at the Library!" Goodness, what could have happened? Did they lift the cash box containing all those nickel and dime over-due fines? Did they steal the entire collection of DVDs? Did someone rearrange all of the carefully numbered books? Or was this just a misleading re-counting of some innocuous event in our little burg in the suburbs?

The statement was made by my wife a few weeks ago, in reply to my innocent question over dinner – "How was your day, Hon?"

Having spent the day at the local library, which is one of my love's clients, she was sharing what had been a highlight of her day. She continued, "Over the last few weeks someone with an artistic bent, but lacking an easel, has taken to using the inside of the Men's Room door to demonstrate their talent."

"You mean graffiti?" I interjected.

"Yes. The Director keeps asking Jack, the maintenance guy, to clean it up. But I think he's us-ing soap from the dispenser in the lavatory to do so, since traces of it continue to be readily apparent af-ter each attack. And then the guy armed with mark-ers returns to update his art!"

My curiosity piqued, and wanting to get right to the heart of the matter, I then asked, "What kind of pictures?"

But I never heard the answer, since the phone rang just at that moment. I think it was my mother-in-law or one of the kid's alumnae associations soliciting contributions. We never did get back to the subject.

That is until yesterday afternoon.

A call came in shortly before five on my "police scanner" (aka office phone). "Grab the belt sander, a paint brush, and the can of polyurethane we used on the picnic table," echoed the familiar voice of the love of my life.

"What's up?"

"Bring that stuff to the Library immediately. I have a job for you!"

A bit confused about the tools and supplies being requested, I hesitated for just a moment. But then, her last statement resonated in my mind. Sensing it was not another "Honey Do" item, but an opportunity for real work...

It was all I needed to hear and I was on my way.

And so it was, armed with the strange set of materials, that the love of my life met me at the entrance of the Library. "They've struck again!"

Noting the blank look on my face, she continued, "Graffiti! It's happened again. This time, however, the tag was different!"

Once again finding a blank look on my face, she went on, "Tag – that's the term for the signature of the graffiti artist. On the Men's Room door..."

"Aha, a copycat crime!" I replied as indication of my understanding of the issue. "This is like an episode of *Law and Order*. All that's needed is Brisco with a groan-inducing joke before the commercial."

She must have known I was trying to come up with some bit of humor worthy of Brisco; but not sharing my whimsical mood, cut me off with, "Don't even try." Focusing instead on the issue at hand she went on, "Fortunately, we beefed up the security in the Library last year."

Hmm, the domicile of our community's great literary works is equipped with security cameras. Am I the only one that sees something wrong with that statement? Is there a concern that someone may steal the entire Biography section? "Oh no, we must have ghosts – all of the 130's are missing!" (For those unfamiliar with the Dewey Decimal System, those are books on Paranormal Phenomenon. Bet even those familiar with the old library numbering system did not know that one!) But, I digress...

Now, the reason for my love's involvement is that in addition to her computer consulting work, she is a bit of a "jack of all trades" at said Library. As such, she had overseen the installation of the security equipment and knows best how to review the tapes of the aforementioned cameras. She thus got roped into sitting with the Director of the Library, Lydia, to watch hours of video taken over the last few days. When it was first installed, I briefly considered offering my services for such a function (I have spent a lot of time in front of a TV screen) but rejected it due to the lack of action – hours and hours of people sitting at tables reading.

Via some fine detective work, they determined that a teenage boy had executed the earlier dastardly deeds. Lydia contacted the police, but they would only take action if the individual was caught in the act – hard to do since it is a single-use lavatory.

Instead, the Director took the law into her own hands and threatened the suspect with the confiscation of his library card if the graffiti recurred. Wow, bet that put the fear of God in him!

But now, newly-signed art was found on the door. Convinced that remnants of the earlier crimes were the cause of this latest caper Lydia decided that another cleaning would be insufficient. The door needed to be sanded down to its core, eliminating all traces of any graffiti. Of course, this being outside of the duties of Jack, the maintenance guy; a carpenter, painter, or some other qualified professional would have to be hired.

And so it was that the aforementioned call came in on my "scanner" last evening.

Now, I had been working on my career search all day and was dressed in business casual, as seemed appropriate. Not realizing that I was being recruited for such a job, I had not felt any reason to change into "work clothes." Wrong!

Upon examination of the door, I found that nearly half of one side had been marked up. This was a job calling for "tradesman garb" (aka work clothes). I returned home in search of jeans and a shirt that would make me look less Bob Dole and more Bob Vila. Hey, appearance is one of the keys to success!

Upon returning to the library's entrance, I saw my wife and a member of the staff having a heated discussion with a group of hooligans. Well, that might be a bit overstated – the oldest of the group might have been thirteen. Listening in, I heard that they had been making a lot of noise in this traditional sanctum of peace and quiet. Thinking my manhood might lend some credence to whatever threats the women were making, I continued to stand behind them making like I was there in some official capacity – exuding male dominance.

Not sure if I had any impact, especially since I was not exactly wearing FBI garb. Nevertheless, after the kids were reprimanded, and all dispersed, I delayed heading off to my task. Instead, I took up a position near the book stacks reading a newspaper, doing my best imitation of an undercover cop intimidating any potential "criminals" with my mere presence. My cover was blown when "the boss," otherwise known as the love of my life, reminded me of what I was there to do!

Comfortable that the threat had passed, I headed for the Men's Room to attend to my carpentry duties. Lydia asked that I not take the facility completely out of use since it gets a lot of traffic. Hmm, I was to address the problem while the door remained in place. Not sure, but was I expected to relinquish the room if anyone had need for it? I never got the opportunity to find out.

Propping the door open, I hooked up my power sander to an outlet across the hall from the lavatory. I then pressed it against the door and turned it on. Fine wood dust started to fly everywhere!

Within a minute alarms started blaring throughout the library! Aha, I was sure those troublemakers had tripped off the alarm.

As I raced out of the lavatory, with the sander in hand, I felt the glares and pointing fingers of the staff standing at the circulation desk. It was only then that I realized that it had been the fog of saw dust drifting in the air that had set off the smoke detector. Dropping the sander, I began waving my arms, in a feeble attempt to clear the air, hoping that would quiet the shrieking klaxon.

Lydia ran past me on her way to disarm the alarm. Then, not wanting to delay further, she used her cell phone to contact the security company to preclude their call to the fire department.

But, alas, she was too late.

Within five minutes not one, but two fire engines, sirens blaring, pulled up to the library. Three ax-wielding, fully robed firemen came bursting through the front doors. Following the pointing arm of the Director, they pushed past me to enter the lavatory to confirm that it was just me, with the sander, who had set off the alarm.

Having confirmed that there was not a bonfire burning atop the lone toilet bowl in the six by eight foot room, they agreed that the saw dust must have set off the smoke detector located just outside the lavatory and they left in a huff.

As the heavily attired firefighters retreated to their trucks, I saw the previously mentioned little hoodlums grinning and whispering. I'm sure they were saying that the "faux cop" was really a poor imitation of the bumbling "Tim, the Tool Man" who had, in similar fashion, set off the alarm. Oh, the humiliation of it all!

It did not take much to subsequently convince the Director that the job could not be done with the door in place.

I enlisted Jack to assist me in taking down the door so I could continue to work on it outdoors. My request for a screwdriver to remove the hinges was met with a blank stare in reply.

How silly of me to think that the maintenance staff of a public library would have some tools – mops, yes; screwdrivers, not so much. Fortunately, Elise had some in her computer tool kit and we got the door down, though it was no small feat. Try to use one of those tiny screwdrivers made for use on a computer to remove a heavy wooden door sometime! I still have the resultant blisters on my hand.

The staff has a small sitting area beneath an overhang behind the library. We set the door upon some plastic chairs that I found there. Jack left me to my labors and then I resumed my efforts to remove the infamous graffiti. I began with #220 grit sandpaper, which has a relatively fine degree of coarseness – it would allow me to just remove the top layer of varnish which I assumed was the surface sustaining the graffiti. But no, these culprits were using heavily penetrating ink that had actually impregnated the wood of the door. I subsequently went to #150, then #100 – increasingly coarse sandpapers.

Somewhere between the #150 and the #100 I began to notice red streaks appearing on the door. Previously, the ink had only been black. Was I uncovering some older levels of graffiti? This was becoming my own little archaeological dig!

But as I drew back to admire my work I discovered the same rust coloration on the sleeve of my jacket. Tracing it to its origin, I found that blood was running down my left hand! Its source was a slash on my index finger that must have resulted from one of the many times I changed the paper on the sander. Though I am sure I had felt it when it occurred, I am not that immune to pain, I assumed I had ignored it – until I saw the crimson on the door.

Drat! More delays and I had yet to get the polyurethane applied!

Fortunately, the first-aid kit at the circulation desk was fully stocked. With Band-aids applied, I returned to my labors. Soon realizing that it would take something just short of a router to remove the marker stains from the wooden door, I headed home once again to get some very, very coarse, #60 grit paper. According to subsequent research, this level is comparable to that found on a jeweler's grindstone – it could cut diamonds! At that time, though, I was merely thinking, "the coarser the better."

After inserting the new paper into the sander, I proceeded to take off more of the ink – and much of the door to boot! At this rate, another five minutes and I would be removing the letters M, E, and N which were stenciled on the opposite side of the door! Convinced that I had as much ink removed as was possible, I was ready to apply the polyurethane.

Purposefully ignoring the instructions on the can, "Apply only if temperatures are above sixty degrees" (it was then in the upper forties and getting colder by the minute) I popped open the can. My confidence took a hit when I found that there was barely enough in there to cover the portion of the door that I had sanded.

I had a choice. Either apply a very, very thin coat to most of the area recently sanded and hope it would blend in nicely with the old, or buy more and then perhaps sand down the entire back of the door, enabling the polyurethane to uniformly cover the door. This was becoming a larger project than I had the enthusiasm to tackle. Perhaps wood finishing is not a livelihood that I should pursue.

Fearing a directive to head to a hardware store, one with late hours, for more varnish, I elected not to discuss it with "the boss." In fact, she had by then left the library to catch the opening game of the latest round of the NCAA basketball tournament. I was left with the accusatory staff and the "oh, so capable" maintenance guy to weigh my options.

I plowed ahead. The thick, translucent fluid went on slowly.

Unfortunately, though I was outside, the patio had poor airflow and the fumes began making me woozy by the third brush stroke. Amazing, but that little touch of nausea helped the work look better and better as I continued to apply the finish!

The job was finally done around nine. After stopping at home to clear my head and settle my stomach with a late dinner, I returned just before Jack's tour ended at ten. I would need his assistance in putting the door back up to greet those in need the following morning.

Upon examination, I found that the polyurethane was still sticky, but assuming it would dry in the much warmer interior of the library, I enlisted Jack's help and we returned the door to its hinges.

Once in place, it didn't look so bad. I just had to hope that no one would knock too hard to see if the lavatory was occupied. They might end up putting a peep hole in the door!

More importantly, I hoped the graffiti artists would notice how well their artwork had been removed. Perhaps they would be dissuaded from further attempts.

Resting at home later, I began to think that maybe wood finishing might not be such a bad career, though I would have to get a large box of Band-aids.

The sun was shining this morning and the temps were projected to go above sixty. I had just begun to wonder if I should recommend to Lydia that a second coat of polyurethane be put on the door when the phone rang.

Oops, just heard Elise on the phone with the Director – wait, no, cannot be. The Director must be clairvoyant.

The boss hung up before I could ask her to relay my suggestion. Instead she turned to me and said, "That was Lydia. She told me to have a new door installed – a metal one with a special finish that enables a quick cleaning of graffiti."

"Oh, like the back door that I put up last..." I began, only to be cut off.

"And you are not in the running for the job."

No mention of what the Director thought of my work was duly noted. I am sure it had nothing to do with her decision.

Regardless, I will continue my career search today. However, I may leave "wood finisher" in the category of "only if desperate."

Sports Handicapper

Woohoo! March Madness has finally come – and gone. No, not the misdirected frivolity caused by temperature swings that enable you to play golf on Monday, only to find yourself shoveling snow on Tuesday. Rather, the insanity I reference here is that which is commonly associated with the college basketball championship playoffs that close out the first quarter of each year.

The NCAA tournament covers three separate weekends and provides a sports fan's bridge between the Super Bowl and the opening of the baseball season. Since professional hockey and basketball get little attention in this household, March Madness is the "celebration du jour." (Pardon the French – I watched a foreign film last night and am still feeling a bit cosmopolitan.) Indeed, this period of reckless behavior has provided an opportunity to examine a potential career – that of sports handicapper!

Our televisions have been tuned to the games since their commencement two weeks ago, right through their completion the night before last.

I have gotten a lot of reading done.

My business partner, aka wife, aka "Commissioner of the office pool," has been in seventh heaven! She runs our local version of this gambling vehicle via the Internet. Unlike most office betting pools, those participating do not necessarily work here – otherwise the winner could be decided by a coin toss between me and "the boss." This year, vying for a rather lucrative winning pot, were more than sixty participants! Resulting from the classic "six degrees of separation" I might recognize ten by face, and another five by name; the bulk of the bettors are complete strangers – the kids have a vast network of friends.

Adding to this year's excitement was the fact that one of our children's alma maters had made it all the way to the "Sweet Sixteen." Why should they not? After all, five of the schools attended by the six kids frequently compete in the tourney.

"Sweet Sixteen," what a cheesy name. Even my daughters refused to have a birthday party the year they could get a driver's permit because it carried that moniker. Yet, here it is, the objective for a bunch of juiced up, sweaty college guys.

Oh, for those not into college basketball, "Sweet Sixteen" refers to that set of the original sixty-four teams that make it to the second weekend of the tournament, which is affectionately known as the "Big Dance." Are you getting a sense that college is one big party?

The winners of the "Sweet Sixteen" go on to the "Elite Eight," whose victors then proceed to the "Final Four." The last weekend hosts the Semis and, finally, the Championship – both of which are a bit of a letdown on the run of alliteration.

While my love's pom-poms have been waving in the den, I have limited my enthusiasm to frequent trips to the Internet to check my status in the pool, for indeed I joined. I had to – did I not mention that "the boss" is the Pool Czar?!

Now, you may be familiar with these "pools" – every office, schoolyard, and Internet site has them.

You enter by filling out an entry form that looks frighteningly like the decision tree diagrams last seen in a college probability course – the mere thought of which makes my stomach turn. Printing the online form took me several attempts. It kept spilling over onto two pages until our technical support group (aka wife) reminded me to switch the print layout from *Portrait* to *Landscape*. (I didn't know one had to be an artist to succeed as a computer consultant!)

Trying to select the winners in all sixty-three games, when a single loss eliminates a team from further contention, can be quite daunting – if you follow college basketball, which I don't. I've participated in several of these pools in the past, all with no good result. My selections were based purely on who I might have heard had a good basketball team in the last thirty years, or had a good football team, or had a catchy name like GONZAGA!

Now that I finally had the time to give it proper attention and research I was confident that I could finish first or second, either of which would assure me a good return on my five-dollar entry fee.

And so it was that three weeks ago I set out to make my picks.

Amazing how someone with a fragmented knowledge of basketball could sit back upon completing the spider web-like form and muse, "I could actually win this darn thing!" Sound familiar? I am positive that everyone who plays has the same thought.

First, I had to determine who was playing whom. Fortunately, with the assignment of the sixty-four teams to their various brackets, every newspaper, sports Internet site, and brown paper bag (well, maybe not the latter) carries a copy of the brackets with each team's win-loss record and "seed." That last term may need some explanation. The seed is the ranking of each team in the one of four regional tournaments in which it is placed.

The NCAA has the best team play the worst team – how's that for fairness? The second-best team plays the second-worst, and so on, until you finally get to the two most closely ranked teams playing in the eighth game.

Have you got all this?

Two hours into my research and I was flummoxed. I was floundering in statistics about strength of schedule, power ratings, conference tournament results, and which coaches were on their second or third marriages! I was tempted to just go with reckless abandon and select the higher seed, or favorite, in each game. But then I remembered that was how I selected my picks for the last two pools and they each netted nothing more than the loss of my entry fee.

No, this would require me to be much more astute. Back to the research.

Now, how much weight should I give to how well each team has done in the tournament over the last ten years? Wait a minute. Don't these college kids graduate in four years? Why value a team's performance for anything beyond the last three tournaments? And even then, only if a preponderance of the team has remained together. So much for that statistic.

Next I turned to looking into each team's RPI. Prior to this exercise, I had always thought RPI was a renowned engineering school in upstate New York. But not here. No, this is college basketball's

Ratings Percentage Index. Not content to just accept the crazy set of numbers, I did some exploration into what was behind these fractional numbers – you see, no one gets above a one.

Aha, no problem. It appears that the basic RPI formula is a quarter of the team's winning percentage plus a half of their opponents' winning percentage plus a quarter of their opponents' opponents' winning percentage. Got that? Financial statements for huge corporations are more easily understood. Who actually computes all of this stuff? I concluded that the RPI, too, was a set of statistics that left me twisting in the wind. If I was to win this pool, I would have to come up with some other means of assessing the talent.

Feeling my energy level starting to decline, I went in search of a snack in the "company cafeteria," perhaps there are some donuts there. Hey, that's why they have extensive buffets and restaurants in all of the casinos in Las Vegas. You must maintain your strength if you are to be successful in the world of big time gambling.

One Reuben sandwich and two cups of coffee later, I was back at my computer handicapping the various teams in the tournament.

Selection of winners based on the win/loss record of the coach of each team seemed to be a way of tracking some consistent success over a period of time. But then I discovered that most of the coaches had accumulated their records over a series of different colleges! Should I discount records outside of their current schools? Of course, that severely restricts the percentages of those "successful" coaches who had, as a result of their achievements, been hired to coach at bigger and better (aka wealthier) institutions of higher learning.

Oh boy, I was getting a severe case of heartburn. Not sure if it was all of the statistics or the sour dill pickle I had with my sandwich!

This was becoming real work.

It occurred to me that I needed something unique to set me apart from the crowd. After all, everyone and their brother were probably looking at many of these same statistics. If I was to succeed as a sports handicapper, I had to find some way of selecting teams that would become my very own secret method.

After careful consideration, and eliminating the options of color of uniforms, number of married students on the team, and the number of children in the coach's family, I came upon one that had merit.

And no, though quite appealing, I only briefly considered the attractiveness of the team's cheerleaders. That would require a high degree of subjectivity. This was to be a vehicle where I could utilize my finely honed computer skills and program a set of objective evaluators.

I elected to go with team nicknames!

With great fervor, I jumped into the task. Did you know that there are over one thousand schools in the National Collegiate Athletic Association? Not only that, but they utilize more than four hundred nicknames. My head started swimming with Wildcats, Panthers, Bulldogs, and Eagles.

I envisioned a pecking order based on the strengths of each. Hey, it may sound crazy, but I have a ten-year-old niece who won our weekly football pool twice last season using exactly this selection method! Is it not obvious that Bears will regularly beat a trail-weary Cowboy? And those black-feathered Ravens will never have a problem with those yellow-bellied Orioles. Now, exercising some astute intelligence, garnered from years of life experience, I merely had to decide whether a Bison would beat a Ram and how that victor would contend with a Spartan.

Hmm, this was going to be more of a challenge than I thought. Not far into my research, I had to figure out what some of the nicknames even were. What are a Hoya, a Jasper, and a Maroon? (Yes, that last one is not just a color but also the nickname of the University of Chicago.) Then, while a Cardinal surely outranks a Monk, how would the latter do against a Missionary? And which is mightier, a Crimson or Garnet Tide? And I presume Bearcats would beat Bearkats for no other reason than the fact that the latter cannot spell!

This was taking a lot more effort than I had expected. But then I realized I did not have to create an auto company just to win a soap box derby. Rather than tackling the entire set of NCAA schools – I could do that later, I merely had to address the sixty-four teams in the tournament. Now, how would a Hoosier do against a Zag? And a Terp against a Mountaineer, or was that a Musketeer? I was beginning to think that going with the favorites might be a lot easier.

At last, I made it through the list. The first set of battles was difficult enough. However, after determining the "stronger" beast, or character, of those thirty-two games, I had to address the next sixteen. By the time I got to the last fifteen games I was on a roll. I had decided that humans (Mounties, Pirates, and Governors) would readily succumb to wild animals (Tigers, Wolverines and Gators). And they all would eventually be done in by the supernatural (Blue Devils)!

For more information on my tout sheets, go to my newly developed website – sportshandicapping-withanedge.com; it will be up and running soon.

My final selections were submitted to the online pool well in advance of the first game. Heck, I must have had it in at least two hours before the initial tip-off!

Well, after the first two rounds, and forty-eight games, I sat with only thirty-one wins – or, more importantly, in forty-fourth place out of the sixty-five players in the pool! It went downhill from there. Though my Devils did well, they did not take it all. Numerous losses in the early rounds left me bringing up the rear in the final standings with a paltry thirty-seven wins!

Guess I will eliminate sports handicapping as a possible career. Wonder if I can get back my deposit on that website address?

Wait a minute. Did I just hear that Brett Favre is going to try still another comeback? Where are those football pool entry sheets?

Baker

Yesterday was the birthday of my wife / boss / partner-in-crime / soul mate. Having plenty of time on my hands I was able to shop ahead of time to enable said celebration to be a happy one, both for Elise and me.

Gift ideas are not really a problem since I traditionally use that day to give her a jump-start on the new summer line of clothing. It allows her to keep the local charity's clothing bin relatively full. To ensure success I follow my time-tested process of buying presents for her: a) purchase several colors of the same items; b) acquire multiple sizes of the same items; and c) save all receipts – ensuring that everything can be safely returned!

With gift shopping behind me a few days ago, I decided to undertake something I have not tackled in all our years of marriage – making her a birthday cake. Now, I am not embarrassed to say that I have done plenty of cooking over the years, but baking for some reason has always eluded me. How difficult could it be? Hey, could be a way of testing out a new livelihood – baker. (I could then make my own donuts...)

The idea first occurred to me while my love and I were out grocery shopping, a rare joint activity. Wandering down the baking goods aisle, I took the plunge. "How would you like me to make a cake for your birthday?"

Basking in the glow of what I felt was her admiring gaze (or was it severe doubt?) I began weighing my personal favorite options – yellow cake with milk chocolate frosting versus a vanilla-frosted chocolate cake.

Elise must have guessed what I was doing and volunteered, "How about making something I like? Maybe a devil's food cake smothered with dark chocolate frosting. How deliciously decadent!"

Horrors! I hate chocolate-on-chocolate anything. Thinking this was surely an excellent excuse for a leave from the constraints of the South Beach Diet I pleaded, "But since I will be the one eating most of it…"

But no, she played her trump card, "Whose birthday is it?"

Hoping for one last consideration, I weakly mumbled, "Yeah, but who's going to eat it?"

Folding like a cheap suit, I picked up the devil's food cake mix but sneaked in the slightly lighter milk, not dark, chocolate frosting.

As such, early yesterday afternoon I commenced my latest career exploration. The box of cake mix made it seem relatively simple. The right size pan, some water, vegetable oil, and eggs were all that was needed. Whipping out my trusty twenty-five-foot tape measure, I went in search of the requisite nine-by-thirteen inch pan. (Wonder if Betty Crocker kept a tape measure on a tool belt under her apron for just such occasions?)

Like a mad scientist in a laboratory, I carefully measured each of the ingredients. Oops, perhaps I should not have poured the oil right over the mixing bowl – though, the bit extra might enable me to slide the resultant cake out of the pan more easily. And so what if there were now a few egg shells in the mix? Perhaps they will add some calcium – and don't women over forty require more calcium in their diet?

The next step was to blend the contents. Should I do it by hand or use the huge *Sunbeam Mixmaster* – the one that makes rare appearances, usually around the holidays when cookies start appearing in every container in the house? Loving all things mechanical, I elected to go with the latter.

You may be familiar with the device; it's the one with the shiny silver beaters that pop out dripping gooey, but tasty, batter – right into the hands of the kids, who always seemed to get there just ahead of me! I found it buried in one of the kitchen cabinets and almost got a hernia lifting it out. Fortunately, residing next to the monster was a small, portable model. Assuming that this would be a lot easier to clean when I was done, I grabbed it and tossed it onto the counter.

Figuring out how to jam the stupid rotary blades into the mixer was a challenge – they have a particular way of locking into position to keep them from falling out. I pushed and shoved those suckers before finding the "release" button that also allowed for easy insertion.

Prior to starting it up, I noted that there are several speeds on this particular beater, seven to be exact. As the box suggested the beating be done at "medium," I interpreted that to mean four on this specific tool.

Then, leaving nothing to luck, I set the timer on the microwave oven to ensure I blended the contents for the proper amount of time. With beater in hand, I commenced blending the mixture for the requisite six minutes.

My left hand held the mixer and controlled the speed, the other was busy scraping the sides of the bowl while blending, as directed by the cake mix manufacturer – not sure why, but who am I to challenge the experts?

But, soon after beginning, something happened that was not mentioned on the box. The bowl began to move while the mixer was in operation, and, of course, it was making its way to the edge of the counter! How was I to control it since both hands were occupied?

Always the innovative one, I took this as a challenge to be met with a unique solution. Using my hip, I just pressed against the bowl as it made its way toward me. This seemed to work.

Not content to stand there idly scraping and mixing, after a couple minutes I began to play with the speeds like a driver in the Indy 500 – up a gear, downshift two, up a couple, wipe the side, "fold" the mix – this was proving to be the proverbial "piece of cake!" (Excuse the pun – I just couldn't resist.)

At last, the timer went off and it was time to take out the beater blades. I downshifted to zero – failing to do that once when making mashed potatoes created a real disaster. I gently lifted them out of the silken brown mix.

Noting that I had a veritable feast on the beaters for subsequent consumption – no kids to beat me to them this time – I remembered that I was dieting. My conscience insisted I should exercise control. How much of this sweetness would I allow myself to indulge? Perhaps I should put some back into the bowl.

As such, I turned on the mixer to spin off some of the excess.

WHOA!! The darn blades went from zero to five hundred RPM with the mere touch of a button. Chocolate batter splattered everywhere – all over my shirt, along the ceramic tiles at the back of the counter, and as far as the stove top, five feet to my right! Of course, the brown speckles on the white tiled floor could always be attributed to mud; but, knowing my reputation for honesty, I would readily give that up. My simple little baking venture was to now become a major cleaning project! The beaters got ejected into the sink.

Pouring the batter into the pan and baking it was anticlimactic, though I did wrestle with the oven temperature and amount of cooking time. The box indicated that I should bake it at three hundred and fifty degrees for thirty minutes – simple enough. Except then they toss in the caveat, "these may vary due to height above sea level."

Now, we don't own waterfront property nor do we live atop a mountain. I am not really sure of our elevation, so I was a bit concerned about which ways, if any, I should amend the temperature and time. In hopes of lessening my chances of burning the cake, I went with a lower temperature and longer time of baking, since I still had plenty of cleaning to do!

Most of the next hour found me on my hands and knees. This was really frustrating since our friendly little cleaning lady, Maria, had made her weekly visit the previous day. (This luxury began when "the boss" began booking large hours of consulting time, and she traded off the added income for the new expense. Fortunately for me, we did not revisit the issue when my income dropped to zero and my time at home increased dramatically.) The whole time I was on the floor I was trying to figure out why I just didn't get the traditional ice cream cake for her birthday!

No sooner had I dumped the dirty water from the bucket and returned the mop to its home then the timer went off. Recalling my wife inserting a slim wire device into a cake to see if it was done, I searched all the drawers for just such an instrument. Failing, and not wanting to let the cake cook too long, I opted for a wire coat hanger.

Having straightened out the curved end, I tentatively plunged it into the midst of the cake though I feared that doing so might cause the nicely crowned cake to collapse. When it remained "inflated" I remembered that it was a soufflé that one had to be careful not to collapse. (Impressed? Don't be. I have never seen my love make a soufflé, nor have I ever eaten one. I think I saw it on the Food Channel during a weak moment while channel surfing.)

Upon pulling out the hanger, I realized that I had no idea what I was looking for. Maybe this was to allow the cake to breathe. Electing to believe that was correct I took my makeshift poker and proceeded to pepper the cake with spike marks.

But my baking venture was far from over. Who serves an unfrosted cake? Especially one that now had a surface that looked like a recently aerated golf green?

After the cake had cooled, and the floor had finally dried, I was ready to frost the first fruit of my budding baking career. That and the addition of a few sprinkles would be just the right touch. "Writing" with a squeeze tube was not an option – I know my limits.

The frosting went from the can to the cake easily enough. Grabbing what looked like a shiny spackling knife from one of the drawers I applied the putty-like substance to the cake. But then I went to open the little jar of sprinkles.

Elise and I differ in our preference with regard to these tasty little morsels. I favor the "jimmies" type – they look a bit like metal filings. She, on the other hand, prefers the tiny beads which, as I have subsequently found, are referred to in the baking industry as "nonpareil sprinkles." Again, deferring to her on her birthday, I had magnanimously bought the latter.

These little candies must be quite dangerous when used improperly, for they come in a jar with a top that defies opening. I have had medicine bottles that were easier to open! Failing to open it with my bare hands, I tried the "rubbery flap-gripper." (What are those things called anyway?) The top still would not budge. I then rummaged through the kitchen drawers in search of the metal gripper, the name of which also escapes me but every kitchen has one buried in their "miscellaneous" drawer. Failing to find it, I retrieved from the garage my version of those grippers – the good old vice-grip pliers; nothing like the "right tool for the right job" to make it easier.

Except that this might not have been the "right tool" for this particular job.

Adjusting the jaws to what I thought was the appropriate opening I squeezed the pliers a bit too much and... crushed the top of the plastic jar! Candy beads flew all over the newly washed floor. Even my beloved "jimmies" would not have rolled as far as these dangerous little ball bearings, all now lying in wait of an accident. Getting down on my knees for the second time in less than an hour, I scanned the floor in an effort to get every single one.

Thank God the cabinets acted like backstops, or I would still be searching for the stupid pellets. And no, not a single one landed on the cake! Fortunately, there were still plenty left in the bottle to be strewn over my freshly frosted masterpiece. I could have used those picked up from the recently washed floor, but I elected to go wild and just toss them out. After all, they were just those "beads" and not the highly valued "jimmies."

Feeling creative, instead of carelessly tossing them over the cake's surface, I carefully dropped them in such a way as to spell out *ELISE*. I knew better than to try for *HAPPY BIRTHDAY!* And besides, once she saw her name, I assumed she'd figure out the occasion.

At last I was done. I set the cake aside to await the grand presentation. It would then be adorned with several candles and accompanied by a rousing rendition of Happy Birthday, sung in several different keys!

Well, the cake went over big. I even discovered that I like devil's food cake with milk chocolate frosting, though I don't think I would have liked it had I gotten the darker chocolate topping. That said, nearly an hour of flossing that evening confirmed that I still hate those stupid little nonpareil sprinkles!

In fact, the result was sufficiently good that I am reconsidering my life-long profession that I don't like desserts. (Note, donuts are officially not considered a dessert!) Of course, if I do, it will only be those made by someone else. As good as the cake was, it just wasn't worth the effort.

Oh well, so much for baking as a career option.

Though wait, I wonder if making ice cream cakes falls within the realm of the "baker." I did briefly work at an ice cream parlor while still in high school where they sold such delicacies.

May have to keep this option open...

Dog Trainer

This past weekend we ventured up to Connecticut to spend the Easter weekend with my wife's sister, Regina, and her family. It was to be a good chance for all of us to relax and catch up on what has been happening in our lives since we last gathered during the Christmas holidays. My mother-in-law accompanied us. Unexpectedly, it turned out to be an opportunity to take another step in my career search. However, rather than a progressive one, it was to be one of elimination. I found that I am just not destined to be a dog trainer.

Mom brought her little Pomeranian, Chiara, along with us. This is significant in that Regina also has a dog, Rudy, who happens to be a brother of Chiara. Both were adopted, shortly after their births, some twelve years ago. However, having been separated at birth, Mom's has been groomed like nobility, taking on the sobriquet of "the little Princess," while her brother has remained "good ol' Rudy."

Pomeranians are supposed to be intelligent, eager to learn, and very loyal to their handlers. As such, on prior visits in which Mom and the Princess have accompanied us, a great deal of the time was spent on comparisons of the two siblings. Their progress in doing such things as answering to the call of their name, sitting when told to sit, and responding properly when asked if they would like a treat were fully explored.

Having spent too many years teaching our kids to respond properly to these and other similar commands, I've never been too interested in watching the four-legged version. However, being the good guest, I always feigned interest and passively observed the ongoing "dog shows." And, while I thought their responses were comparable, Chiara always seemed to come out ahead in the eyes of the judges. Not a surprising result, since I often felt the panel was more interested in currying favor with Mom than objectively assessing the performances of the canine brother and sister!

This whole fascination with the defenseless pets' achievements has always amazed me. Never having owned any animals, or even inanimate objects as companions (hey, remember the pet rock craze?), the need for their masters to draw parallels to their own sibling rivalries and other traits of humans simply boggles my mind.

Whenever asked if our household had pets, I always answer that we were too busy raising kids – there was no time for animals. And quite successfully, I might add – it has been years since my youngest son, Kyle, last peed on the kitchen floor!

Assuming this weekend would not be much different, other than the fact that the two dogs were now battling more with age-related ailments than learning new tricks or each other, we were met with a surprise that would prove me wrong. Being introduced to this normally high-strung environment (Regina and her husband, Tom, are card-carrying Type A personalities) was another dog – a seven-week old Labrador puppy!

Tom explained that a friend is the owner of two Labs, a male and female. It seems she did not fully succeed in keeping them apart during one of her, the dog's not the friend's, semi-annual times of heat. A lengthy discussion ensued over the question of whether these "events" took place two or three times each year. (I then realized I was in for a long weekend of veterinary education – a possible new career path?) Not actively taking part, I instead ruminated over what happens during these time frames. Do the dogs get all gussied up for a canine evening on the town? Do they ask their owners to step out and leave them the run of the house for the evening? Are there candles involved?

Returning to the issue at hand, yet not having a position on the subject but wanting to show some interest, I questioned why the previous owners would have had a male and a female dog in the first place! Doing so, did they not suspect some dalliances would take place at one time or another? Even I would have expected as much and I, as mentioned earlier, have never even owned any pets. Dohh!

Ignoring my question, Tom explained that the "parents" were a Black and a Yellow Lab. Sadie (who comes up with these names?) was one of the Yellow offspring, though her seven siblings were black, yellow, and chocolate. I began to wonder if we were talking about dogs or cakes. (Yes, black is a variety of cake, as I found last week when shopping for a yellow birthday cake for one of my sons. But I digress...)

Fortunately, no one had suggested that Mom also increase her little "family" by adopting one of the remainder of the litter. Just witnessing the two breeds together for the weekend would be challenge enough.

For those not familiar, Poms, as Chiara and Rudy are called in the trade, are tiny, fluffy dogs.

Small wedge-shaped heads, pointed erect ears and a feathered tail that fans forward over their back gives them a truly regal, or as some might say, pompous look. Lively little dogs, they're strong willed, bold and sometimes temperamental – even in their senior years. In short, based on my familiarity with Mom's dog, a more appropriate description would be "little yippy dog."

Now, Labrador Retrievers, on the other hand are solid, muscular dogs. With a short, hard, water-resistant coat they are loving, affectionate, patient dogs who crave human attention and like to play. All of which seemed to accurately describe Sadie.

Per some site on dogs that I subsequently found online, "If properly introduced, Pomeranians may get along with other dogs without any problems, but some of them seem to think they are much larger than they actually are and do not hesitate to attack much bigger dogs." The latter segment seemed to have been written with Chiara in mind.

Lively and good-natured, the younger pup seemed anxious to play with her two new friends. Unfortunately, she had not read the aforementioned web article, as it quickly became apparent that the elderly pair were not in a frolicsome frame of mind.

In response to Sadie's attempts at play were the snarls and yips of "the Princess," or the appearance of the tail of her tamer brother as he merely sauntered away. It may have been nothing more than the age gap, but it became readily apparent that these dogs were not looking forward to a social weekend.

After a few moments of the canine version of, "getting to know you," I found that our visit was to provide more entertainment than just observing the dogs' interaction. We were to witness the house training of the new puppy! Put this right up there with having eaten bad fish or witnessing a rumbling, though not yet erupting, active volcano - all potentially painful and all subject to unexpected spurts of activity!

The new dog did have an innate understanding of chasing a ball thrown across the floor, though she often slammed into a wall as she attempted to stop on the highly polished floors. What she did not fathom was that she was to approach, if not knock on, the back door to be let out when she had to relieve herself.

The older dogs would waddle to the door if Mother Nature called, but not Sadie. Cries of, "Grab her, she looks like she has to…;" "Oh, oh, too late!" and, "Get the paper towels!" were heard often during the weekend. Perhaps bladder control is something that comes (and goes) with age.

For seemingly long periods, often in retribution for some such transgression, Sadie would find herself in her cage. Don't know if it was the confinement, but frequently she would let out a whimper, which was subsequently interpreted as a warning of her impending "urination." As I was to observe, kids "pee;" but these dogs water the floor and it is called everything but that! In fact, Tom got up twice during the first night we were there when he heard such whimpering one floor below where he slept. (Didn't realize he was such a light sleeper. Next time we visit I will be careful not to flush in the middle of the night.) Not sure if Sadie then "urinated" on demand or if he arrived late each time – I was hesitant to ask the following morning over coffee. His sour mood was a clear indication that his love of the dog had not yet overcome his sleep deprivation.

And thus, the training of the young pup continued. I never knew a dog could have "too much to drink," though I have friends who have that problem. Yes, several times Sadie was yelled at for drinking some of the other dogs' water.

Now, I would have assumed she did so because she was thirsty and not just to aggravate her new companions. However, I was told that the reprimands had something to do with her learning which bowl belonged to her. I really think it had more to do with the frequency of having to "take her out." But what do I know? I never had a dog...

As for the bowls, it turns out that Chiara's is a dainty, gaily decorated pink dish, and Rudy has a green one with his name on it – did they really think the stupid dog could read? Of course, the bowl that Sadie was to use was also green and had her name clearly imprinted as well, but I think she was still working on her letters and had not yet progressed to putting them together into words.

Did these people forget that we are dealing with animals here?

On Sunday we were going to have an outdoor Easter egg hunt. But after witnessing the number of trips the dogs made out to the yard, the love of my life succeeded in convincing all to have the hunt take place in the house, instead.

Nevertheless, later in the day, it was found that someone had tracked in some "deposits" from an earlier excursion.

No one would own up to it. Furious accusations of each of the dogs by someone other than their owner were accompanied by equally fervent defenses. "Not Chiara, she was over near me sleeping." "Not Rudy, he was drinking from his bowl over here." Of course, no one was defending the poor puppy, but a physical check of her paws and bottom by Tom convinced all that it was not her.

I later found damning evidence on the sole of one of my shoes, but I was not about to step up to the plate. I might have been banished to the rear porch for the remainder of the day. A quick swipe with a paper towel and all traces of my guilt were gone.

Now, Tom and Regina are most gracious hosts. There is always an abundance of delicious, gourmet food. But it was difficult to enjoy the meals on this visit, as poor Sadie was frequently being lectured about the need to stop gnawing the edges of the area rugs or the legs of the dining room table. A few times I even stopped in mid-chew to see if it was me who was causing the tension level to suddenly escalate in the room. Most of the time I was able to carry on without further pause. At one such moment of silent angst, I turned to the love of my life to obtain confirmation that I had not just used the inappropriate fork – only to find that Chiara had just passed a bit of gas!

All in all, it was a happy and joyous weekend, right up to playing games following dinner on Sunday. That said, it was a bit difficult playing *Trivial Pursuit*, while Tom and Regina were in the midst of an unending round of "Sadie Pursuit."

The drive home was uneventful. We only had to stop once to let Chiara "run amongst the bushes."

That is a dog owner phrase for what the rest of us would call "taking a dump."

In retrospect, perhaps the attention paid to the dogs during the weekend was a blessing – no one seemed to notice the gravy stain on my tie that I did not discover until after we arrived home Sunday night.

We got home early enough for me to view some of the day's golf tournament, which I had recorded earlier in the day. Those guys make it look so easy – if I just work on my putting, might I be able to make a living playing golf? God knows, it has to be a lot easier than dog training.

Oh, and by the way, I was so proud of my boys who were with us this weekend. Neither one was hit with a rolled-up newspaper and neither one "peed" on the floor!

Linguist

Last night, after months of serious, alright, maybe somewhat serious adherence to the precepts of the South Beach Diet, I had a strong craving for Chinese food. Not the stuff we used to make – some chicken, vegetables and teriyaki sauce tossed into a wok and presto – instant Chinese food! (That was good enough when there were a ton of kids living at home and we attempted to convince them it was genuine Chinese.)

No, I was looking for some serious, MSG-laden Chinese take-out. Little did I know that it would lead to the elimination of still another potential career path for the next stage of my life – in spite of the fact that I have a real passion for Chinese food!

Getting the boss' agreement that this minor transgression would not set me back several months in my efforts to lose weight turned out to be the easy part. In reply to my suggestion she answered, "I had a late lunch with some colleagues – I'm not really interested in dinner anyway." That left just Adam, and he will eat anything on the table – the flowers in the centerpiece are always in jeopardy!

With the green light given, a tear came to my eye with joy. I rummaged through the company archives (also known as the folders in the cabinet beneath the phone) to find a menu for one of the three Chinese restaurants in our small town. Not that there are that many folks of that national origin in the area; I just think it's indicative of how much cooking is going on in suburbia today. So much for those fashionable cook books and cooking shows on TV.

Fond memories swept over me as I rifled through the folder's contents. Ah yes, the pre-South Beach Diet days when the answer to, "what's for dinner?" was often, "Whatever you feel like ordering!"

Rapidly did I skip over the menus from *Domino's, Boston Chicken, Taco Bell, The Golden Bear Miniature Golf Course* (must remember to use that free game, if I can only find three others willing to pay full price...) At last, there it was, our favorite Chinese restaurant – *China 4.*

Yep, that's it. No *Peking Hunan Wok* or *House of Chan*; nope, just plain old *China 4.* Is there a *China 1, China 2*, and *China 3*, you might ask? Not in our town, I can assure you. The others are the *Green Jade China Inn* and the *East Broadway Chinese Restaurant* (now there's a catchy title). Who christens these places with such names?

Anyway, scanning through *China 4's* extensive take-out menu – it was four pages long (can they really offer all those dishes?) – I elected to go with the *General Tsao's Chicken.* (Wonder if there ever was a General Tsao? And if there was, what did he do to warrant having a spicy fowl dish named after him? Did he win the Battle of the Hot Chili Pepper or was he the Secretary of Defense in the Ming Dynasty? Forgive this last bit of meandering – can't help myself, I love history.) Adam was easy, he opted for the same.

Dialing the restaurant resulted in getting someone that pronounced "China 4" with the fully-expected heavily-Asian accent. I asked for two

General Tsao's, one with plain white rice and the other with pork fried rice. I much prefer the latter, but "the boss" was standing next to me and I was not about to completely abandon the South Beach Diet with her in range of hearing!

My request was met with, "What numbahh, what numbahh??"

Doing some quick translation of her dialectic Chinese (might it be Mandarin?), I assumed she was referencing the demarcation on the menu. What is it with the menus in these restaurants and their insistence on numbering all of their choices? Their use of alpha-numerics, associating columns A, B, C, and D with accompanying numbers one through thirty, is mind-boggling. I recall being in one such restaurant and being instructed by a waiter, "Select one from cowum A, one from cowum C, and one from cowum D to get special rate." I used to think this was some Chinese thing, until I realized that they don't even use our letters and numbers in China! Who is really behind these restaurants, anyway?

Recouping from my reverie, I registered that I had to provide her a "numbahh." I quickly rattled off, "C11 with a D2 and another C11 with a D3," subsequently hoping I had not misread and inadvertently ordered the *Kung Pow Chicken*.

As I was confirming my order combination, she fired off her next question, "Pickup or delivuhh?" Now, there was no way I was going to be able to not only convey my address, but also how to get here. I've been through this before – "Drive past the library... No, not fast and scary, I said past the library!" Instead, I elected to pick it up myself and said as much. This only led to another request for, "Numbahh?"

Ignoring her request, I rattled off, "One with plain white rice and one with pork."

Which only brought another request, "Numbahh?" Since I could not think of a better reply, I fell back on the old, "C11," though in a higher volume.

Her frustration with me was evident as she then shouted, "Foan numbahh!"

Ah yes, having mastered these calls in the not too distant past, I knew then that this was not a request for something off the menu, but rather the point on the communications highway by which I might be contacted, which I readily provided.

But then I was shocked when she said, "Mistahh d wok, twenty minutes." It wasn't the time that surprised me – it takes a while to properly prepare *General Tsao's Chicken*, but rather the fact that she knew my name, or at least I think that was what she was saying.

It then occurred to me that they must have access to a computer with a reverse telephone directory! And yet, if that is the case, why don't they use an online map service to find my house, which is just this side of the library?

Not wanting to continue this linguistic wrestling match, I thanked her and hung up, dreaming of piles of *General Tsao's Chicken*, with those fiery little hot peppers, on a plate laden with rice. (Is your mouth watering? Or is it still morning – in which case, put this down and return when it is a bit closer to dinner time.)

Not being able to restrain myself, a mere fifteen minutes later I walked into the little restaurant. Actually, to call it "little," or even a restaurant, is a stretch. Other than the kitchen, it has nothing but the pickup counter and maybe three tiny Formica-topped tables. I was greeted by a perky little Asian woman standing next to the cash register, with her back to the kitchen. But rather than the expected "Good evening," she said, "Numbahh?"

Oh no, my little friend from the phone. Suddenly I felt like I had entered a foreign country and forgotten how to communicate. Again not being sure if she wanted my phone number or the number of the items ordered, I blurted out, "Two *General Tsao's Chicken*. One with plain white rice and one with pork fried rice."

Thank God, it must have been a slow night, or not that many people share my love of the spicy chicken dish. She replied, "Ah, Mistahh d wok!" like we were long lost friends. She then shared another of her recently learned phrases, "Ten minutes," smiling the whole time.

How could I object? They were clearly in control of my dinner with their sizzling fry pans and kettles of boiling rice sitting atop massive stoves with flames that seemed out of control. Patiently, I turned away to stand by one of the few tables and began to scope out the place.

Two of the walls were plastered with glossy, but faded, photos of the various items on their extensive menu – each of which looked surprisingly like the other. I briefly wondered which was the *Moo Shoo Pork*. (I've always loved the name, but have been hesitant to waste a meal on something that might turn out to be roasted pig's hooves.)

Then I turned to admire a huge painting that occupied the better part of the last wall.

The fresco was a pastoral scene of what appeared to be a Venetian gondola floating down a river bordered by mountains that looked like the Rockies. Then again, based on the cone shaped hats sitting atop those in the boat, I quickly assumed this was a scene from China. (Or Vietnam, or Cambodia, or you fill in the blank with some Asian country). As I was attempting to decipher the locale, an elderly Asian man, perhaps the owner or manager came over to "chat."

"I from there," he proudly said, pointing to the mural.

Aha, the classic "restaurateur" coming out from the kitchen to mingle with the guests. He probably saw this on *Restaurant Wars* and figured it was a good way to ensure repeat business. And there I was – a captive audience.

Not one to mind a little schmoozing, I figured, "oh, what the heck." So, innocently enough, I offered up, "Where is that?"

I think he then said, "Fiji."

Now, I am not the best with world geography, but isn't Fiji an island in the South Pacific, with palm trees and long white beaches? This scene had huge, rocky mountains (no pun intended). So I elected to explore a bit further and risked a guess, "Where in China? Like, how far west from the Pacific Ocean?" (In retrospect, I realize that this was like asking someone from St. Louis how far they are from the Atlantic Ocean! Dohh!!)

Anyway, he seemed to graciously accept my inquisitiveness and, after thinking a bit, answered, "Maybe twenty-four hours by train."

My brain then went into overdrive, trying to compute where that might be, thus leading to some other interesting question on my part. Hey, Barbara Walters I'm not. Perhaps my face conveyed something else, as he then quickly added, "But trains in China are very slow, there are lots of people."

Now, the first part caused me to immediately rethink where he might be from; the latter I figured was just a freebie in case I was a total idiot.

I then ventured, "Is that near Tibet?" a country I thought to be near China.

To which he merely smiled. (Why did I not go with Boston Market when I had the stupid menus in my hands?)

Reaching deep into my limited knowledge of China, I then tried, "How 'bout with regard to Shanghai?" (When I get nervous I start dropping syllables. That must really help foreigners understand our language.)

In reply he said, smiling, "Near Hong Kong."

Now, I am not positive, but isn't Hong Kong famous for their harbor? Which happens to be on the Pacific Ocean? Or should I get a new map of the world? And if I am right, then how could it take twenty-four hours by train? I've heard of the "slow boat to China," but this train must be setting new records for slow speeds! Or was he telling me that Shanghai is near Hong Kong?

Mentally resigning, I then began smiling as he was and just admired the picture with him. Guess it was just a slow night, rather than General Tsao's lack of popularity, since no other customers came in to distract my host.

As I was about to ask some other inane question like, "Is the water in China wet like it is here in this country?" the cheerful woman behind the counter mercifully called out, "Mistahh d wok?"

Never has such a mispronunciation sounded so good!

I bid my host farewell with a bow. (Not sure why, but I always feel the need to do this when in a Chinese restaurant – or whenever speaking to someone who appears to be Asian.)

Turning my attention to the young woman, I passed on the offer of duck sauce. Our dinners had been tastefully placed in a brown paper bag – ah yes, more fine "dining-in" at company headquarters. Not wanting Adam to be disappointed if they were not there, I peaked inside to ensure that we had gotten the requisite two fortune cookies.

Satisfied that it contained all we ordered, I paid for the cuisine and turned to leave. Passing my newest friend, I bowed once again, murmuring something like, "It was nice talking to you."

He replied with what sounded like, "You come again. I show pictures of family in China."

Dinner went well. Unfortunately, even with a freshly printed college degree, Adam could not come up with any better explanation or identification of General Tsao. Though he took an Eastern Religion course in his third year there were no military leaders mentioned. That was money well spent!

I attempted to relate to Adam and Elise my conversation at the restaurant, only to have her suggest that I never did have an ear for languages. "Don't consider a linguistic career, it would surely be short-lived!

"Did you already forget the Wongs?"

Ah yes, the Wongs. They were a family who used to live across the street. Ming was the head of the family. He and I would often run into each other while walking to the train in the morning. Being friendly neighbors, we would chat the whole way. However, though they lived there more than four years, for the life of me I never understood a word he said; nor, I am sure, him me. Yet we smiled and laughed a lot.

I wonder if the restaurateur at *China 4* is related to Ming Wong.

Probably not since, like he said, "There are a lot of people in China!"

Career Counselor

Yesterday, I had a bit of a *Through the Looking-Glass* experience. After months of searching for a vocation that will address my passion, I was called upon to do some career consulting by the love of my life. Wanting to provide me with an opportunity to capitalize on my recently gained knowledge, she suggested that I might want to take on some work she had been requested to do for one of her clients.

With little else on my calendar, I readily agreed. I looked forward to reaping some financial reward for my months of intense study and research. "You did make sure the guy is going to pay for this service. You know it's not really consulting if you don't get paid for it; right?"

"Oh, definitely, though I did quote her a slightly lower fee since this was your first venture in this arena. Her name is Sister Margaret Clement of Cheroux." The expression on my face conveyed total shock. "Oh yeah, did I mention that the client is a nun?"

I barely heard her as she continued, "She was the Coordinator of Student Volunteers at some small college but she's now out of work since her funding grant was not renewed. She told me she had spent the majority of her career in various fields of education, but was now seeking something different."

Before the train got too far out of the station, I blurted out, "I didn't even know nuns had careers – other than being nuns." Suddenly this "opportunity" looked like nothing more than a chance to fail. "What the heck do I know about nuns and their career ambitions? I didn't know they did anything but pray and teach Sunday school!"

"Oh, give it a shot. What else do you have going today? She's already insisted on paying for your services – oh yes, I mentioned that you knew all about surfing the Internet for opportunities. If it doesn't go well, you will have wasted nothing more than a couple hours of your valuable time," the last part dripping with sarcasm.

Though not being a big Shakespeare fan, she then hit me with something that must have been in the prior day's crossword puzzle, "As Hamlet said to Ophelia 'get thee to a nunnery'." (Hmm, must think about doing fewer *Jumble* puzzles and more crossword puzzles if I am going to gain a foothold in her company.) And so I did go, though in this case the nunnery was a comfortable two story duplex in residential Queens.

Ringing the bell, I fully expected to be greeted by some meek little woman robed in black with rosary beads hanging from her hand. Instead, I was surprised to have the door answered by a dignified, well-dressed woman who could have easily passed for a senior executive at a Fortune 500 Company. After going through the usual introductions Sister Maggie, as she insisted I call her, invited me into her home. Tastefully furnished throughout she led me into the living room, where I was directed to a seat on the couch while she sat on an arm chair across from me. For a moment I thought she would offer some snacks (maybe a donut or two?), but no, it was right to business!

Not exactly sure of what I was there to do, I recalled the classic definition of a consultant – one who borrows the client's watch to tell them what time it is. As such, I asked, "Sister, how is it, exactly, that you would like me to assist you?" I had hoped to fit "professionally assist" in my opening question, to ensure that she would understand that this session was being done for a fee, but failed.

"Well, I've been looking for a job for a few months and am becoming overwhelmed with the process.

"Before leaving my last position, I sought out the assistance of the university's outplacement center. I was hoping they'd provide me with the tools to facilitate my search via the Internet but all they gave me were several pages of web sites to peruse in way of finding a position.

"Then, not to say she was not encouraging, but the woman I dealt with warned me that few, if any, jobs are found via the Internet. She told me to network, network, network!"

All of this sounded so familiar. I was tempted to ask if she had worked on her "two minute intro," but elected to pass for fear of sounding too cynical. Besides, the duplex only had two floors – not much chance to use her "elevator speech" on random strangers.

She then continued, "Well, that's what I've been doing; calling everyone I know, but to no avail. So now I would like to try the Internet and those sites she suggested. But I don't know enough about the computer to do so.

"That's why Elise was here – to set up the PC. Then, as we were talking, it came up that you might be able to assist me."

108

Okay, Consulting 101, now that the client has clearly defined her requirements, where do I begin? "Do you have a résumé?" I asked.

Moving to what appeared to be a hutch in the dining room she began rummaging through a drawer. She brought back to me a three page treatise on each of the positions she held over the last thirty years. Supposedly, this had been approved by the career office. As I flipped the pages she asked, "What do you think?"

Not being a speed reader, I spent at least ten minutes digesting the myriad details printed in a very small font. Her "Statement of Objective" – "Getting a position with [name of potential employer]" was not exactly a show stopper. The remainder of the content was great if she was seeking a position as a religion teacher in a parochial school or a social worker.

Unfortunately, she was not. "Been there, done that" was her reaction to my suggestion that she seemed a shoe-in for either of those positions. No, she was looking to "explore new avenues."

Skipping the last page's "Workshops Attended," I gently suggested, "It has merit but might need a little tightening up."

Perhaps reading my body language, she interrupted my stalled train of thought. "Your wife told me that you too had recently left a lengthy career – one in finance?" (Recently? Wonder how else "the boss" had portrayed her consulting partner?)

"She mentioned that you've been looking into alternative careers as well – perhaps you could share some of your experience with me."

Here is where my tap dancing began. I have become rather adept at this as the subject of my "current occupation" has come up frequently in recent social conversation.

Tempted to ask if she was into home or automotive repairs, I instead explained, "Yes, I have been doing some serious inventorying of my personal skill sets, in hopes of finding a career that might optimize those talents. Perhaps you too should review your professional life to date and extract those skills which might be portable and have value to a potential employer." (At this point, I felt so good with my dancing that I wondered if she could hear the taps on my shoes!)

But, rather than commence work on an exploration of her attributes, she asked how long I had been at this and how it was coming along. (Suddenly, my tap dancing reverted to a Moon Walk! I needed to back up this train of thought.)

"Well, it has been a bit longer than originally planned. But a working spouse has allowed me the luxury of delving deeply into a different aspect of the job search – one that involves an exploration of one's likes and dislikes. The objective being to find that for which one has a passion." (As soon as that word slipped out of my mouth, I realized that it might have been inappropriate with a woman of the cloth. Though I did not know what vows she had taken, I felt confident that "passion" would be in conflict with one of them!)

Quickly recovering and trying to move on, I continued, "There are a number of resources for doing an inventory of those skills and personal preferences, such as the Briggs/Meyers Test."

Sister Maggie then demonstrated one of her strengths by graciously correcting me, "Oh, I used the Myers-Briggs Type Indicator extensively during my years of social work, though I preferred Jung's Gestalt personality theory..." She went on, but I kind of zoned out and focused instead on the fragrance of chocolate that was drifting in from an adjacent room.

A bit of silence stirred me from my trance. Realizing that she had finished, and comfortable that the conversation had left my personal job search, I decided it was time to leave the skills inventory issue aside and return to the search. I suggested we move over to the desk upon which sat her PC. (Reluctantly, on my part, for in leaving the comfortable seating I felt I was abandoning any hope of tasting those brownies whose smell had been wafting into the room since my arrival!)

"How about you boot up the computer?"

Much to my surprise, I then watched her fingers dance merrily across the keyboard. Though elderly, there was no sign of arthritis here. Then again, I observed that either her dexterity was lacking or she is a terrible speller. It took her three attempts to successfully log in! (Reminded me of a typist I once knew. Her mantra was "speed or accuracy, I can't provide both!") Sister explained that she shares the computer with the other nuns with whom she lives. Can the security of their computer use be that big an issue?

Finally arriving at her personal home page, I was relieved to see it was YAHOO and not some Vatican-sponsored web portal. I then suggested, "Shall we visit one of those job search sites you mentioned earlier? They have huge numbers of job listings. Why don't we register on one and look it over?"

She keyed in the first web address and I pointed out that they had more than a hundred thousand jobs listed. Sister exclaimed, "God has answered my prayers!" But then, she had been overwhelmed with the numerous listings in the New York Times. "How will I ever find the time to look at them all?"

"Well, it's probably safe to assume that you would not be interested in most of the jobs listed. However, with the use of some of their filtering tools, we can narrow the search considerably."

Presuming that she was not interested in relocating, I pointed out the location filter. Selecting New York State narrowed the opportunities to less than twenty thousand, but Sister was still feeling overwhelmed.

"Perhaps we should narrow the search even further by selecting the city of New York." The number dropped to less than ten thousand. (Guess there must be a lot of opportunities in upstate New York. Too bad the weather is so bad or I might consider relocation.) Further exploration of that specific set of filters indicated that we were including such places as Brooklyn and Staten Island since they are boroughs of the city.

"Oh, but I'd not be interested in jobs in the entire New York Archdiocese! I would not want to work in the Bronx. Could we somehow limit it to just the Rockville Center Diocese and perhaps the Queens portion of the Brooklyn Diocese?"

I knew then that I was in trouble. How does one explain that as robust as these search engines are, breakdowns by Catholic regions would probably not be available? I suggested we use still another filter category.

"Click on the option labeled Job Categories."

Opening up that filter revealed over thirty different choices. Figuring this might shed some light on just what she was interested in, I asked her to select one that might fit her interests.

"Non-profit sounds like a good category." (Guess poverty must have been one of the vows she took. I was glad I did not ask her to filter on salary range.) Much to my surprise, over two hundred positions came up with twenty-five listed on the first page.

"Perhaps you might like to look at a few of them."

The third one down met with, "I could never work at St. Gregory's. I hear the conditions there are deplorable. There is a lot to be said for quality of life, you know." (Hmm, must remember to have her share her thoughts about employment conditions at our company HQ. I have yet to get that bulletin board in the snack room, aka kitchen. The number of holidays in the company has never been discussed. And, the lack of donuts is ridiculous...) Oh yes, sorry, where were we?

After she had scanned several of the opportunities, I elected to continue with my demonstration of the various features on the site. I pointed out that there were sections that would assist her in the aforementioned skill assessment, as well as the preparation of a good, working résumé. Here I stumbled a bit, but recovered well. I explained that while her current one was good, a more abbreviated one might get better reviews and work better for online applications. But, just as I had her go down the third step in the thread of résumé preparation, she looked at her watch and abruptly changed the subject.

"My apologies, but I have an appointment that I must get to. I promised to bring some brownies to an after-school program where I volunteer."

Alas, my consulting session was coming to a rapid end. Had I succeeded? Was she pleased? Would she graciously accept my bill for services rendered? I quickly ran through my mind what we had done and wondered if I could legitimately charge her anything for the time we had spent together. Had I provided anything of value? Should I chalk this up as "pro-bono" work, though I'm not sure if that applies here, since I only hear it used by lawyers on TV shows. What would "the boss" do in this situation?

As I stood to don my jacket, Sister asked, "Oh, there is one thing I would like you to look at before you leave. Elise was unable to take care of it when she had last visited," and then, very demurely, "it may require a man's touch."

Anticipating that we were about to get into the world of home repairs, I readily agreed to do whatever I could.

"Could you set the clock on my VCR? I am tired of seeing the dashes displayed and can't set it to record anything in advance since the time is not set." At which point she trotted into the living room and whipped out the manual for the VCR.

A full fifteen minutes later I was still finding out why my love had been unable to fix the problem. The manual referenced a menu that was to come on the TV screen, but I could not get it to come up. I checked every wire and jack in all of the associated equipment, knocking down a framed picture that was resting next to the TV. She picked it up, commenting, "Oh, it was an old one anyway."

Sister was now frequently checking her watch but I did not want to admit failure. After a bit more exploration, I realized that the piece of equipment on top of her DVD player, the one I was fixated on, was not a VCR but the cable box! The digital clock was on a combination VCR/DVD player. I had merely to switch the TV setting from *DVD* to *VCR* in order to get its related clock menu to come up on the screen. Alas! Success!

"Oh, God bless you. I knew you could do it!"

Unfortunately, as I started to set the clock, it only drew her attention to how late it was and that she was now running late. "Thank you so much. Just leave it there, and I will finish it later."

But, being the professional that I am, I insisted that I could do it quickly and did so. Of course, I am not sure if I left it on Daylight Savings or Eastern Standard Time. Oh well, if I get a call from her the first week in November I'll know just how to fix it.

With little time left, Sister expressed her thanks and asked that I send her a bill in the mail. (I half expected that she was going to bolt out the door leaving me there in front of the TV.) I eyed the brownies in her hands, but since she did not offer me any, I merely bade her farewell and offered continued assistance if needed. She nearly ran me over as I headed out the door.

Driving home I tried not to focus on the delectable little chocolate tidbits that had been so close and yet so far. Perhaps I should stop and grab a donut on the way home. But no, it was important to get back to my job search. Instead I thought about what I should charge. The career counseling, coupled with two dollars, would get her a ride on the New York City Subway.

115

However, I did get the clock on her VCR working. Hmm, how many indulgences could that be worth? Think I'll leave the billing up to "the boss" — she has more experience with it than me.

As for me, I must get back to my own career search. Hey, with enough practice I could possibly turn such research skills into a paying career.

Landscaper

Well, another potential livelihood has been buried – that of landscaper. This is one that I should have dismissed years ago when I errantly tried to use a chain saw to trim my shrubs. At the time, I was gainfully employed and not searching for a new passion in life, I was just another weekend warrior doing his chores who had mistakenly substituted the tool normally used to cut down trees in place of the hedge trimmer which my neighbor had borrowed. This latest epiphany was the result of that which occurred late last week, in which I was a participant, though I would have preferred to have been a spectator.

Spring has been awakening with a roar. The increasing temperatures have me once again thinking about getting outside to work on the yard. What is it with suburbanites and our fascination with lush green lawns? I'm convinced it's a conspiracy hatched by the grass seed and fertilizer industries!

At least once or twice each summer, my neighbors' emerald green lawns have prompted the love of my life to question my landscaping skills. Jealously would I admire them as well and wonder if I was using the wrong fertilizer, not watering sufficiently, or not talking enough to the little seedlings as they pushed up from the ground.

But now, being around a bit more than in the past, I have finally uncovered the means by which they've achieved their success – lawn service companies!

The last week or so I've seen myriad gangs of migrant day laborers working on the small patches of yards in the neighborhood. The success of those *Home and Garden* covers was due to these little groups of landscapers, though "yard workers" is a better description, doing all kinds of wonderful things. And they begin well before the grass starts to grow in earnest.

And so it was late last week that I decided it was time for us to get a lawn service.

Well, maybe not for the entire season, but just long enough to get the grass up and running. You know, have them do the hard part and then leave the rest to me. After all, I can run the automatic sprinkler system with the best of them. I just need them to come and do whatever it was I saw those guys doing that earlier morning. No silly rakes for them – they were pushing machines that looked like oversized lawn mowers, though there was no grass yet to mow. How much could it cost to get one of those crews here for an hour or so?

A phone call enabled me to find that they were "thatching" and it would "only" cost two hundred bucks to have my "massive" estate done! That was the good news. The bad news was that they were booked for the next two months. Several more calls found similar results.

Then I got a bright idea. Why not rent one of those machines and do it myself?! A call to a rental company confirmed that the equipment to do so was available. Though there was rain in the forecast, I planned to rise early the following morning and rent the machine. I would do the day laborer thing, fertilize, and then mix a batch of Margaritas – all before the rains came.

Unfortunately, I awakened to a gray sky and a fine mist falling. Drat! "Why didn't I do it yesterday?" I moaned to myself.

"Because all major projects look better with the light of a new day and I really did not know how long it was going to take," came back my snippy retort.

While I stewed over a breakfast of soggy raisin bran, "the boss" noted my sour mood. Knowing of my ambition for the day, and perhaps to rally my spirits, she offered, "Hey, it really hasn't rained enough to be a problem. You should go ahead as planned. The latest forecast is that the heavier rain is not to come until late today. I bet you can have it done in no time."

Being the good corporate citizen, I accepted the challenge and off to the rental shop I went.

Not really sure what I was looking for, I timidly approached the front counter. "I need to thatch my lawn. Do you have the equipment that I need?"

The crusty old guy behind the counter smiled at my obvious lack of knowledge of all things mechanical. "The tool you need is called a power rake. I have several available.

"What size do you need?"

Gulp!

In reply to my blank look, he continued, "Well, how long does it take you to mow your lawn?"

This was a tougher question than it sounded. It's been fifteen years since I last mowed my lawn. No, the grass has not gotten out of control, but it's been that long since I convinced my first son that it was "cool" to operate a large piece of power equipment. After passing along such sage wisdom to his younger brothers, I am only now facing the task once again, as my last born is not planning to move home after finishing his last year of college and Adam is always on the road with his tours.

Forced to take a shot in the dark, I shook myself from memories of days past and replied, "Uh, about two hours or so." Actually, even this seemed a bit much, but I did not want this guy to think I had a miniscule piece of property!

"Hmm, the Model 850 should be sufficient. It'll cost you two hundred for the entire day. But, since you probably have a fairly small piece of property..." Darn, he had seen right through my ruse. "You can have it for two hours for eighty."

I was afraid to ask what the cost would be if I were fifteen minutes late on the return! "I think I can do it in the shortened time frame. Where is it?"

"Well, first I'll need your credit card to put down a four hundred dollar deposit. And then I'll need two forms of identification."

Along with my credit card, I handed him my driver's license and, not having my passport or any other type of ID available, my blood donor card. But no, the latter wasn't a sufficient secondary form of identification! He suggested that I bring in the insurance card from the car. (Heck, you don't need that much proof of ID to buy a new car!)

Fortunately he did not notice that the insurance card was out of date. "Now, you just need to sign this form and initial the box if you don't want the insurance – I don't think you'll need it."

Not wanting to prolong this little meeting, I did as told.

After agreeing to forfeit my firstborn if I didn't return the equipment on time, he directed, "Drive 'round to the back of the store. The fellas there will show you how to use the 850 and load it onto your truck."

"Uhh, I don't have a truck. I thought it would fit into the back of my van."

"Oh yeah, no problem, just go 'round back and they'll get it in I'm sure."

Well, "the fellas" turned out to be one little Hispanic kid who could not speak English. The "850" looked like a snow blower on steroids! Fortunately, it was started with a pull cord, a method with which I am familiar, for beyond that the kid was useless in explaining how it worked. Hoping I could figure it out myself later, we hoisted the behemoth into the car and I raced home, knowing that the two-hour clock had begun ticking!

Unloading it was another story. Except for the love of my life, there was no one to help me get it out of the van. Confident that I could not lift it on my own, I reminded myself of that which I always told the boys, "Use brains not brawn." Standing there pondering a solution got me nowhere, and I could feel the costly minutes ticking away.

Finally, I came up with an idea.

Retrieving two eight-foot two-by-fours from the garage, I would create a ramp from the back of the car to the ground upon which I could just roll that big boy right on down. A regular genius! (Perhaps I should consider a career in industrial design?)

Sounds simple right?

Question – how does one keep the boards from moving when pulling the "850" onto the boards? Each time I attempted to do so, one or both would slip off the bumper and onto the ground! After several attempts, I finally got the machine's wheels on both boards – only to find that halfway down, the boards were no longer at the width of said wheels. And, once the "850" was rolling, it was not going to be stopped!

With agility that a modern dancer would have admired, I jumped back to avoid the now out of control monster as it went crashing to the ground. I wondered how much of the four hundred dollar deposit I would get back if I returned it, within the allotted two hours, but in several pieces. Maybe I should not have been so cavalier about foregoing the insurance.

Having examined it to make sure that no parts had fallen to the ground, not really being capable of much more, I was now ready to commence "power-raking." For those neophytes who have never done this, the machine has these vicious little fingers, poking out from a center axle that rotates, which gouge the ground to a depth that you set at the beginning of the task. It reminded me of a dog covering the trail of his recently dropped mess.

The first pass seemed to barely disturb the soil. Not having any idea of what it was supposed to look like, but hoping to see more evidence of my efforts, I increased the depth setting. When I saw soil and grass flying every which way, I decided I had it right and "plowed" into my project.

Not long after starting, I learned that if you stay in one spot for long, the "850" just keeps digging deeper and deeper. Thus it is important to keep moving at a steady pace, which was easy in the beginning, but – did I mention this thing was HUGE? The more I did, the slower, though straighter, I moved.

At one point I paused a bit longer than I should have. Hmm, wonder how deep a Koi pond has to be? And would Elise like one in the middle of the front lawn – perhaps if I make it a Mother's Day gift?

Racing (everything is relative) around the lawn (the clock was ticking!) I completed the whole "estate" with over an hour to spare. With so much time already paid for, I decided a quick circuit with the lawn mower was called for – it would pick up all of the turf tossed about by the "850." Then I could give the lawn one more going over with the rental. After all, at these rates I don't plan on power-raking again for a long time to come.

Pulling out the mower from the shed was the easiest part of that job. This is one of those types that has a "power drive" so you don't have to push it. A lever marked with a rabbit and a turtle presumably indicates two levels of speed, which I further assumed was the rate of rotation of the blades. Since I wanted maximum suction, I opted for the speedy hare.

Unfortunately, I quickly learned that the lever with the animals controlled not the blade speed, but the rate at which the wheels turn. Having set it at the rabbit instead of the tortoise I had to sprint to keep up with it! And the mower was not sucking up a thing!! Why did I have to spoil those boys with the fancy, smancy model instead of the old push-type of mower? Or had it been a Father's Day gift for me?

Not having the time to do the necessary technical review of all of the levers and buttons on the mower (who knows where the instructions are hidden), I called for reinforcements. Catching her just as she was leaving to visit a client, the love of my life quickly figured that in addition to putting it into drive I had to hold down another lever to engage the blades. Proof once again why she is the computer hardware expert in the business, while I am periodically engaged to do only programming work! There was no stopping me now.

With the sun now bursting through the clouds, the temperatures rising, and the clock ticking, I chased the mower around for another twenty minutes followed by another round of power-raking. What had been a rather sad-looking lawn, now looked like a battlefield in a World War Two movie! Oh boy, hopefully I could get the fertilizer down and the grass growing before the love of my life returned!

As the time wound down on my two hours, I was confronted with getting the "850" back into the car. I lined up the boards like I would line up a ten-foot putt on the eighteenth green at Augusta. I could not afford to have it fall between the boards this time! Pushing it up, I realized one board was slightly off, so I reached down to push the "850" to the left a bit and felt a surge of pain in my hand! I had gripped the one spot on the engine that, I subsequently saw, had a label on which was written: *Caution: HOT when operated!* Now blistered, I ignored the pain and forced it the rest of the way and tossed aside the boards. I was a man racing the clock!

Arriving at the rental agency with a mere two minutes to spare, I rushed into the store and pushed my paperwork across the desk – only to be told that I could not check it in until it was unloaded from the car and inspected by the fellas in the back!

Finding Armando, or was it Luis, lounging in the back, I quickly popped the back of the van and asked that he "inspect it." He lifted it out on his own – I was now handicapped with blisters on my hand and rising blood pressure. He then proceeded to perform an inspection that appeared to be limited to ensuring that it was in one piece!

Racing back to the front desk, I found the old codger I had dealt with earlier. He was explaining the proper use of a "power thatcher" (I guess when you ride on it, that's what it's called). His audience was a dapper-looking yuppie, dressed in a white sweater, neatly pressed brown slacks and expensive Gucci loafers. I wondered if the dude was also going to negotiate hiring the fellas in the back to do the work. My gruff old friend was graciously showing him a rather colorful brochure providing operating instructions. (Were no such aids available for the "850" two hours ago?)

Clamoring for his attention, I started tapping on my watch with my blistered fingers. He finally came over and checked me out by stamping my rental agreement. (I found it interesting that the only one that got the results of the oh-so-important inspection by Armando/Luis was me!)

Retrieving my deposit, I returned home only to be confronted by a yard waiting for another mowing to somewhat improve its appearance. Great!

Once again I found myself behind the stupid mower treading over the "plantation" for the fourth time that morning. With no kids home this summer, I could look forward to facing this task repeatedly over the next several months. And viewing it as just another chore around the house didn't help. Who could I turn to? The boss surely isn't going to do it.

As for the Margaritas that I had envisioned earlier — I never did get to them. Once I applied a salve to each of my burned fingers and wrapped them in bandages, I could not press the buttons on the blender. Each attempt ended up with two buttons partially depressed — the blades failing to move. I settled for a bottle of beer and dropped cashews into my mouth directly from the bag.

Oh, and the idea of landscaper as a career? I think not. That which I had concluded earlier in my life has now been confirmed. It is not for me. Besides, I could never get accident insurance coverage that would be sufficient to cover my efforts.

Volunteer

Since paying careers seem to be few and far between, while searching for them I have mixed in doing some volunteer work. My latest foray into the world of humanitarian endeavors was to become a driver for a program that provides home-delivered meals to people in need.

Wednesday was my first day.

On the previous Sunday a plea was made from the pulpit for volunteers to assist in a rapidly growing organization, *Meals on Wheels*. It appears that as the economy deteriorates the requests for this type of assistance goes up. They were seeking those who could spare one or more mornings a week.

The solicitation fell on my slightly deaf ears. Though between positions, I am too busy in the pursuit of: 1) a second career, 2) consulting work, and 3) addressing items on the infamous "Honey Do" list. As such, the idea did not find fertile ground in the old gray matter and was quickly forgotten.

Exiting the church, a long-time acquaintance caught up with me in the parking lot. Armando quickly asked how the kids were doing. Having had all six go through the church's grammar school, this is a common Sunday morning conversation starter. I gave him the five minute rundown, wanting to get to the bagel shop before the rest of the congregation who were now rapidly exiting the lot.

127

Not wanting to be totally rude, however, I then made the requisite inquiry about his family though not daring to ask by name or even implying that he even had kids, since I am never sure who in the parish had what.

He mumbled something about Tony working for some accounting firm and then, "The other one, the bum, is still out of work!" Smiling, but not wanting to prolong the conversation out of fear he might give me the same classification based on my employment status, I asked him to give them both my best and started for the car.

But then he grabbed my arm. It was apparent that he had something more on his mind than just exchanging family news.

"Did you hear Father talking about the *Meals on Wheels* program?"

Being well before my first cup of coffee, I quickly ran through all I had heard in the previous hour or so in church. Matching bits with what Armando had said, I tried to recall if the readings addressed some prophet's wheels taking him into Heaven. Or was there something in the sermon that concerned wheels? And why was he quizzing me here in the parking lot? Was he trying to determine if I had been one of those nodding off during the first Mass of the day?

Not waiting for an answer, he continued. "They got a pretty good operation going down there. *Meals on Wheels* is a really good organization. The food is actually pretty decent. And, boy, there is a really hot blonde chick who runs it."

Normally, such conversation might get me listening closer – food and blondes are two favorite topics of mine. But it was still on the dark side of eight in the morning and I really don't know Armando well enough to be discussing his personal preferences in women.

About to beg off, I then heard, "You still got connections in your old company, right?"

Fretting he might next ask if I could assist "the bum" in finding a job, I replied, "Well, it's been a few months now. I have been busy exploring other avenues."

"Well, maybe you can..."

Oh no, had word spread that about my extensive research on the subject of potential employment paths?

At that point, I looked up to see my love wildly waving to me from the car, indicating a strong interest in getting home to some freshly brewed java. Gesturing that I was coming, I bade Armando farewell and told him I would think about it, though I was still not really sure what I was to think about.

Shortly thereafter, safely seated in our sun drenched kitchen, sipping my coffee and noshing on a freshly buttered bagel, I was skimming through the church bulletin. After determining that we had once again not won the weekly raffle, I flipped through the various articles found therein. Following the usual perusal of who was getting married, who had died, and who had been baptized, I was about to move on to the Sunday comics. But then my eyes fell on those recently heard words, *Meals on Wheels*. Figuring this was what Armando was chatting up in the parking lot, I read further.

"NEEDED – weekday drivers for *Meals on Wheels*" it began. The brief item then assumed you knew of the program and merely provided a name and number to contact if you had, "even one morning each week to offer to this most important of charities." Again, my mind came up with several reasons to ignore the request for assistance.

But as the day wore on, the absence of anything more than the crossword puzzle to occupy my mind, the shallowness of my excuses became fodder for strong feelings of guilt. Maybe the words from the pulpit had found a home in my subconsciousness. Before I knew it I was rummaging through the mound of papers left strewn on the kitchen table to find the name to call – I could at least go that far.

And so it was on Monday that I first contacted Erika. Her silken voice was sultry – I readily pictured the blonde locks that Armando had referenced in his brief description. Hmm, maybe there was something to this whole service thing. And, Armando did say the food was good – maybe they fed the volunteers!

Erika indicated that I would first have to meet, and be approved by, Sister (mumbled first name) Dakota, who heads up the program. Picturing some kind, elderly nun, straight out of the movie *The Bells of St. Mary's*, I agreed. Of course, my concurrence was aided by the fact that Erika would be there to walk me through the rest of the process. Feeling the graces building up in Heaven already, I hung up the phone and blocked out all of Wednesday morning on my "busy" mental calendar.

In anticipation of the meeting, I got my hair cut on Tuesday. (It's important to make a good first impression, even in volunteer work.) Indeed, an extra splash of cologne was not inappropriate Wednesday morning, though the day did not start out well.

Wanting to get a close shave, yet using an old blade, I had nicked my chin not once but twice. Drat! And there was not a styptic pencil to be found in the entire house. As such, with small pieces of tissue adhered to various parts of my face I joined the love of my life for breakfast.

"What happened to you? You're bleeding like a stuck pig!"

Hmmff. "Good morning to you too!

"I just had a little accident with the ol' razor. As soon as the bleeding stops I'll remove the tissue."

"Okay... and what about the bleeding ear lobe? Here," she continued as she handed me a napkin, "put this against your ear before the blood drips onto your shirt."

I had unknowingly clipped my right ear lobe in one of those vicious swipes with the razor. Not common, but not unheard of – I have somewhat of a history of such wounds occurring, especially when shaving in a hurry.

"How bad is it?"

"It's still bleeding. Keep some pressure on it while I get something to help stop it."

Wanting to lighten things up a bit, I quipped, "Not to worry, I'll be sure to keep it above my heart!"

Returning to the kitchen with a box of bandaids and some antiseptic, she took the red-stained napkin from me. "I couldn't find the styptic pencil. Where do you keep it?"

"Would I be a walking advertisement for Kleenex if I had one?" Boy, I thought, my humor is at the top of my game today – must be the adrenaline associated with the upcoming interview.

Ten minutes later the only evidence of my earlier surgery was a small bandage hanging from my ear lobe. Yet, upon examining her work in the mirror, it looked like I was wearing an earring! I made a mental note to keep my head turned to the side when meeting Erika.

Arriving at the distribution center of the program some fifteen minutes before I was due, I joined what appeared to be a meeting of the local senior citizens group. Picking out the guy who looked the youngest (he had some hair on his head), I asked where I could find Erika.

He turned and pointed out a petite little woman standing with her back to us in the next room. Five-foot-two, if she was that, and not quite blonde hair. Indeed, a faint hint of blue on gray is a more accurate description, (must remember to ask Armando if he is color blind).

Stepping into the room, I extended my hand just as she turned and introduced myself, suggesting that I had possibly spoken with her recently. I was sure she would reply that there was yet another "Erica" that I had spoken to – the young blonde with the sultry voice...

But no, she brightened right up at the memory and welcomed me with a big hug! Erika seemed so overjoyed that I was sure she had mistakenly thought I was bringing some huge largesse of donations rather than just an offering to be another driver for her little group.

After some inconsequential chit chat, she introduced me to several other volunteers, most of who looked like they should not be behind the wheel of a car. Then the little octogenarian pulled me down a hallway to meet Sister Jacinta Dakota. Just as we approached the doorway to an office, out came a vision from my past – a nun actually wearing a habit! But not just any nun...

Sister Dakota had the build of an interior lineman for the Green Bay Packers. Though I had an inch or two on her for height, she packed a bundle beneath those robes that would have made me feel safe walking in any of Brooklyn's toughest neighborhoods.

In way of introduction, Erika greeted her with, "Sister, this is our newest volunteer."

Sister then reached out a delightfully pure white hand that was the size of a pork roast. "Welcome to St. John Bosco's Outreach Program! We are always pleased to get new volunteers."

And then, without further ado, she turned and said, or should I say, commanded, "Please join me in my office." There was no chance that I would not follow in her wake.

Either the office was tiny, or her substantial girth just made it seem that way. Once seated, she pulled out a set of forms that she asked me to complete and sign.

Perusing them, it appeared that I was agreeing to have my background checked by everyone from the FBI to Homeland Security. Mistakenly sensing my hesitation as stemming from anything other than the fact that I am a slow reader she assured me, "Oh, this is routine for all volunteers. You shouldn't feel threatened – that is, unless you have anything to keep you from delivering meals to shut-ins!"

I felt like I was back in the Principal's Office at my parish grammar school. I quickly ran through my mind what type of record would bar me from acceptance – someone caught stealing others' lunches? Content that I had not done that, at least not since grade school, I went ahead and signed the forms.

Sister gave me her blessing (can nuns really do that?) and then shooed me off to Erika's care.

Erika, there was to be no other Erika or Erica, related that she had been running this local chapter of *Meals on Wheels* since retiring twenty years ago. She was proud of how it had grown (an accurate indicator of the economy). She explained that the program helped folks four days a week (I didn't ask what happened the other three days) and then showed me the freshly delivered shrink wrapped meals (looked like defrosted frozen dinners).

After completing her presentation, probably delivered hundreds of times, she gave me my marching orders. I was to pick up a list of recipients, each with an address and clearly marked directions, load up the proper number of meals and be on my way. I would drive to a home, knock on the door, and hand them their meals. That was the sum total of my volunteer responsibility.

Oh, by the way, in person, Erika's voice was not nearly as sultry as it was on the phone. Once again, I was duped by a great phone voice, only to be disappointed by the owner's physical appearance. So much for Armando's hot blonde – must remember to find out just how old he is! Also, there were no "free meals," or even donuts. Indeed, the coffee machine was empty when I passed it on the way out.

134

Having reviewed my list of houses to be visited, I headed for the home of Gunther Hammermill, the first recipient. I noted that his name had a note instructing me: "Enter if no one answers the bell, and call out his name." Sure enough, when I arrived, the door was ajar. I rang the bell and then knocked but got no response.

Pushing the door open, I called out, "Mr. Hammermill? *Meals on Wheels*." After which I spotted an elderly man sitting in a wheelchair at a table in the kitchen, just off the room onto which the front door opened. Following his gesture to come in, I approached him only to find that he was sitting there with what appeared to be a bloody white rag wrapped around his forearm!

"I cut myself coming in here. Might you have a band-aid on you?"

Other than the miniature one hanging from my ear lobe, band-aids are not something I normally carry with me. Loose change, yes; *Tic tacs*, yes; sometimes, maybe even a *Snickers* bar – but a band-aid? Not so much!

Oh, and did I tell you that the sight of blood makes me woozy?

Upon closer examination of his arm, from a distance of about ten feet, what I had thought was a white rag turned out to actually be some crimson stained paper towels held in place by two rubber bands!

Suggesting that I might have something in the car, I quickly trotted out the front door.

Gasping the fresh air, I plopped myself onto the front seat. After what seemed like ten minutes of sitting with my head between my knees, I remembered that we had a brand-new emergency kit in the back of the car. Tearing the plastic wrap off it, I found it had several bandages of varying sizes and... latex gloves! Yes, it is important in this day and age to not get a stranger's blood on one's self. Heck, if there's that much blood, I won't need gloves – a cold compress to help me recover consciousness maybe, but gloves?

Upon reentering the house (did this really fall within my new job description?) I found that Mr. Hammermill had removed his "bandages." He sat there revealing a small gash on his arm. For all I know, the "bloody rag" may have been paper towels that had been used to previously mop up some spilled ketchup. Anyway, I tore open two large band-aids which he then, thankfully, took from me with his good hand and applied himself.

He proceeded to explain that while maneuvering his wheelchair through the doorway, his arm had scraped along the door jamb. After ensuring that he would be okay (he had more color in his face than I had in mine), I bid him adieu and told him I would be back the following week. Once outside the house, I raced to the car.

Fortunately, the remaining client visits were a lot less adventuresome. One elderly woman had a barking terrier that jumped nearly to my chest as I opened the door. Following a shout from its owner, I gingerly pushed it back into the house with my foot before closing the door, having handed the night-gown-clothed occupant the bag containing her meal.

Another stop found a spry, little old Irish guy answering the door in his boxers and T-shirt! "Good morning, what can I do for ye?"

I introduced myself, explaining that I was with *Meals on Wheels.*

"Well, now, aren't ye a handsome young man! My name's Mickey."

Then, eyeing me a bit too long said, "I really like your outfit." (I was wearing a golf shirt and shorts).

There was someone of unidentifiable gender standing further in the house. Wearing a floor length robe, I was not sure if it was his wife or "life mate." But, the gleam in Mickey's eye led me to guess that the robed number behind him was indeed his "partner."

Concerned that he might next ask me to join them for a snack, I thrust the two meals at him, wished him a good day and backed away quickly.

The subsequent trip home was made in record time.

Not sure what next week will bring. I expect I will have the same set of homes to deliver said meals. Hopefully, Gunther will have healed by then; the lady with the dog will have a leash for her little mongrel; and Mickey will have finished dressing before I arrive.

Perhaps I will become a professional volunteer. Who would have thought offering my time this way would be so venturesome? Forget the Department of Labor and its seven thousand positions. I may have to look up opportunities on the United Way site, though the Red Cross and any EMT positions will be promptly eliminated – too much blood.

Appliance Repairman

Adam has been living at home since graduating from college two years ago. He has worked hard to maintain his independence. One manifestation of this autonomy is that he does his own laundry.

Laundry is one of the duties in our household that I have done for a long time. (One must be sufficiently comfortable with his masculinity to say that in public.) With a brood of six kids, it was my attempt to somewhat share the household chores with the mother of my children. As such, I took pride in this reflection of my influence on Adam. That is, until he approached me late last week just as I was having some lunch.

"Uh, Dad, I was doing some wash, and when I checked to see if it was done, I saw some water on the floor. Does that mean there's a problem?"

There is ALWAYS a little water on the laundry room floor – those appliances work so much, I've always just assumed it was their version of "sweat." I was sure this was just an amateur's mistaken concern that there was a problem.

"Nah, that often happens. It's probably just condensation on the concrete floor," I replied and went back to my salami sandwich.

"This looked to be a bit more than just condensation. You might want to look at it."

To humor him, I followed him to the laundry room.

Well, what is normally a bit of moisture was now looking more like Lake Ontario! The washer was rocking like a jukebox blasting out The Rolling Stones' Greatest Hits!

Figuring it was something he had done wrong, I smacked the knob at the top of the washer to turn it off. I was about to grill him about his knowledge of good laundry procedures when I noticed the load setting at *Small*.

Popping open the top of the washer, I found a large quantity of soaked clothing in a relatively low level of water. Presuming this was due to the load setting, I was about to lecture him on the proper evaluation of load sizes when my eyes dropped to the bottom of the machine. I could see that water was still dripping from the bottom of the machine.

Opting to pass on the quiz, I directed him to commence mopping. "Don't restart the washer. In fact, don't even touch the machine. I'll come back later and figure out the cause of the leak."

Feeling pretty certain that the problem was related to his having overloaded the washer, I left him to his labor and returned to the kitchen. Perhaps those pains in my stomach were more of the hunger variety than that of indigestion.

Subsequent to his cleanup and the eventual drying out of the room, I returned to the scene of the crime. I pulled all but a few of his dripping clothes from the washer and piled them in a laundry basket. My first investigative step was to run a small "test load." Don't know why, but I guess I was hoping for a miracle.

The machine filled without any evidence of water leaking out onto the floor. Ah, success.

Perhaps the flood was just a temporary response to his having overloaded the machine after all.

But then the behemoth went into its first drain cycle. Before I could even get out the words, "miraculous repair," I found myself standing in a miniature version of Niagara Falls! Once again I slammed the knob to the *OFF* position – only to watch the water continue to drain out onto the floor. Time to call the appliance repairman!

But wait, I am no longer busy with a full-time job. And those guys charge an arm and a leg just to walk in the front door. Surely, a man of my intelligence and skills could find the source of this leak and repair it myself. Why, an hour or two and I would have it done.

At peace with my assessment, I banned the use of all laundry appliances until I fixed the washer. Not that a formal announcement was really necessary since, as I mentioned earlier, Adam is the only other person in the house who does laundry. And he was more than willing to relinquish this aspect of his independence.

And, thus, I awoke today to attempt my hand at "appliance repair" – perhaps a new career option!

My first challenge was figuring out how to access the "guts" of the machine. The top looked like it would just pop off if I could find the little clips that held it in place. Using a putty knife and hammer as my weapons, I jousted with it for twenty minutes. Minor pieces of white enamel flew into the air as I probed for the right spot.

Conceding that little skirmish, I went to my thirty-year old *Fix-it-Yourself Manual*. I've used this book numerous times over the years, with mixed results. However, here I was confident that, with a little guidance...

After finding the appropriate chapter on top-loading washer repair, I was crestfallen to find the following in the first section: "Many people, thinking the top panel pops up, begin ruthlessly prying on the seam between the top and front panel and only end up with a disfigured washer." Hmm...

Not exactly a stellar start.

Speed-reading my way through the rest of the chapter, I had the shell of the washer off before the morning-radio talk shows had ended. My next step was to seek out water stains as an indicator of the source of the leak.

Searching for evidence of such stains was like looking for dirty clothes in your kid's bedroom – they were everywhere. Fortunately, most of them looked like remnants of the time the drain hose clogged and the water spilled over – another disaster that occurred a few years back. However, being the crack detective that I am, and seeing water still dripping from it, I concluded that the plastic gadget at the bottom was probably the source of my latest "slow leak."

A trip back to the manual told me that the gadget in question was the drain pump. It even indicated that this was often the site of a leak in a direct drive washer. (Don't you just love the technical jargon? The only "direct drive" I am familiar with is that which is hoped for from the tee box on a golf course – though I usually hit a slice...) The project describing the replacement of the pump was rated four stars, meaning that, with little mechanical ability (a given), this was a nearly impossible job.

Never one to be cowed by challenges, I plunged ahead.

Now, don't know about you, but I don't work well in cramped spaces. As such, the leaky trap under the sink and the quagmire of wires behind the television are deliberately avoided. That is, until a higher authority, aka the love of my life, pulls out a sopping wet box of detergent or drops a beloved figurine behind the entertainment center. Well, the focus of my attention today resides in a room not much larger than a walk-in closet. And, it has the dryer and an oil furnace as roommates. While it would have been easier to first move the adjacent dryer out of the room, I determined that if I lay prone in front of the two appliances, with my legs poking out into the garage, I could probably just pull the pump off the drive shaft, as shown in the manual's diagram. This should be a piece of cake.

Getting the two retaining clips off was not too difficult, though there was some blood found at the scene later – subsequently traced to scraped knuckles. But the pump was another story. It was not readily sliding off the drive shaft.

A full hour later, and only with the leverage afforded by two monkey wrenches, a pint of rust penetrating solvent (*Liquid Wrench* to those in the trade), and a screwdriver as long as my forearm, did I get the "easily removed" pump off the machine.

With the newly removed part in my hands, I made a quick run to the appliance parts store. After some genteel opening remarks, I provided the pump to the young kid working behind the counter and asked if they carried a replacement.

"Well, we would not be much of an appliance parts store if we didn't," was his reply. "This is just a basic water pump," showing off the knowledge obviously acquired at his vocational training school.

After consulting a book that was big enough to hold the history of man, he disappeared into the myriad aisles behind the counter muttering some digits that I assumed were the part number.

Some ten minutes later, he handed me a box that presumably contained the proper part and announced, "That will cost you a mere forty-nine ninety-five."

As my mouth dropped, he added, "ah, plus tax."

"A *mere* fifty bucks? How could such a small part cost more than ten percent of a new machine?" I bellowed.

But he would not share in my angst, suggesting instead, "Perhaps you should think of it as ninety percent cheaper than a new machine!" He smiled at his facility in doing higher math! Why wasn't this kid in school, anyway?

Having been one-upped by a teenager who was probably apprenticing to become an appliance repairman, I paid for the pump and returned home to install it. I figured I could have the whole job done by lunch.

Unfortunately, putting the new pump on was twice as difficult as removing the old one. It just would not slide onto the drive shaft (another step that was described as "easy" in the manual). The opening in the pump was identical to the size of the drive shaft and though I pushed as hard as I could, the pump just would not go on.

Applying grease to the drive shaft did nothing but leave my hands covered in slimy goo – which then made the firm grip of any other tool a real challenge. Lying down, I lowered my head to the six-inch height of the shaft to ensure that I had the pump perfectly level before pushing. But even that was done for naught. This called for stronger measures.

It was time to bring out my trusty old hammer.

Maybe with just one good shot...

Oops, that piece of plastic flying out of the face of the pump could not be good. On the other hand, perhaps it was just decorative. At least the stupid pump was now in place. Examining it more closely, I found that through this new hole I could view the inner workings of the pump. And they all seemed to be in good shape. I quickly reinserted the retaining clips and then, with the machine only partially assembled, gave it a test run.

Setting it to a small load level, water flowed into the tub with no problems. But then it went into the drain portion of the cycle.

Oh boy, my feet were now being showered by what appeared to be an open fire hydrant! Water was spitting out from the front of the pump – right at the point of the missing piece of plastic. The impact of my slamming the dial to turn off the machine nearly tipped the washer! I won't share my "expressions of joy" as I mopped up the floor and removed the now broken pump!

Back to the supply house and the wise cracking store clerk.

But no, he was not there. Instead some elderly, professorial type helped me. (He looked like the type of guy who would normally respond to a call for repair help.) Handing him the original pump, I meekly explained, "I was in here a little while ago. I need another water pump, the one I bought earlier may have been the wrong size and it cracked while I was installing it."

Graciously not encouraging me to further expound upon my plight, he just smiled in a fatherly way, the one that smacks of, "children shouldn't play with grown-up's toys," and, without looking up any mystical part numbers, headed back into the aisles to find a second pump.

Upon returning, he sensed my weariness and said, "Looks like you're having a rough day. These things can be difficult to install."

"I'd say so. It was bad enough getting the old one off, but putting the new one on was a disaster. Any suggestions?"

"Well, it's been a while since I was out in the field. Did you try putting some oil on the shaft?"

"Yeah, done that. No luck."

"Well, just make sure it's lined up right and then give it a good push. It should slide right on." I changed my guess about him being a former repairman, he is probably the bookkeeper. But then he continued, "Tell you what, since this is your second one, I'll knock ten percent off the price." Hmm, maybe he is a member of the family who owns the place.

I thanked him and plopped down another fifty bucks. Taking some small satisfaction from the discount I headed back to make a second shot at installing the pump – sans hammer!

The next attempt did not go much better. However, now that I was another fifty bucks poorer, I was a lot more patient. After a lot of grunting and pushing, I got the pump on "close enough." Though not nearly as tight as the original position, I was able to reset one of the two retaining clips. Another test run and there was not only no gushing water, but there appeared to be no dripping. SUCCESS!!

Not content to just run the washer devoid of clothes, I reassembled the entire machine and threw in a few of the clothes that Adam had left in the laundry room from his interrupted earlier foray into the world of laundering. Lacking confidence in my repair skills, he had taken the bulk of his load to a laundromat to finish his domestic task. Grumbling about kids and their tendency to too quickly spend their limited income, I grabbed some clothes from a hamper upstairs to increase the load and ensure a good test.

An hour later I was pleased to see that the washer had gone through its entire cycle without a drop of water hitting the floor! As I smugly transferred the load to the adjacent dryer, I noticed that a few of the white socks now had a pinkish tint...

Oh no, Adam had left a red shirt in with his stuff! Several of my white T-shirts were now a light scarlet. And Elise's favorite white shorts...

I went in hot pursuit of a bottle of bleach!

So much for "professional launderer" as a calling; though I do feel pretty good about my mechanical repair skills. Wonder how well appliance repairmen do? Perhaps I will further explore that as a potential second career.

As for the clothing, I tried to convince "the boss" that magenta is the latest fall color in all the fashion magazines. Judging by the look on her face, fashion designer will also be dropped from my list of possible second careers!

Negotiator

Periodically, the "company" has to replace a member of its fleet of cars. At its peak, when we had several "employees" (aka kids at home) we had three vehicles. We are now down to two. With more than a hundred and twenty thousand miles on the van, it was one of those times.

To many, the turning of the sixth digit to the left on a car's odometer is like a relative reaching the century mark. You are happy for them and consider them fortunate to have lived so many years, but would hesitate to make any long term reservations on their behalf. I, on the other hand, feel that unless the car has completely stopped running, a few more miles can be put on it – regardless of the mileage. But then, I also don't believe in euthanasia...

And so it was that, at a recent "board meeting" (aka dinner), it was brought up that a lot of dollars were being sunk into the van for repairs and perhaps it was prudent to search for a replacement.

With only one dependent child left, and he being away at college, I quickly envisioned scaling down from a van to some small, sporty model. Okay, maybe not a convertible, but perhaps one with a sun roof?

Not...

A review of the minutes of the meeting reveals discussion of the fact that numerous road trips, with several family members joining us, were still planned for the foreseeable future. Though we could

147

take multiple cars, such separation would disrupt our philosophy of "the journey is as much fun as reaching the destination." Reminding me that "the more the merrier" is a favorite company slogan, it was decided that we would spring for another van.

Now, I don't know about you but I hate buying a new car. Unlike purchasing a suit or some good vegetables (I love to squeeze the zucchini) where the posted amount is what you pay, with cars you have to go through the dreaded bargaining process. On the other hand, the "love of my life" looks upon that exercise as an opportunity to get an up close and personal taste of capitalism at its best. Allow me to explain the method used most recently.

First she would do her homework concerning what we wanted in a car (everything that NASA puts on the shuttle) versus what I thought we could afford (have anything with four legs?). In the old days her research was done via consumer rating magazines at the library. While the amount of data available may have been daunting, the "best buy for your money" rating was sufficient for narrowing down our preferences.

The Internet changed all of that. The details about each and every vehicle increased exponentially and the number of "best buy" designations soared. But more importantly, to me anyway, we now had access to financial details not previously available.

The old sources provided a price range within which each car might be acquired. (Does anyone pay the sticker price?) But with the Internet, one can find exactly what the dealer's cost is! (Who is the "Deep Throat" of car dealerships providing this sensitive information?)

Armed with such insider's info, we would head out early on a Saturday morning convinced that we would find our next car, at our price, well before the sun set in the West.

Our method employed the "good cop / bad cop" strategy. (Forgive me; I have been watching too many *Law and Order* shows on TV.) It goes something like what follows.

Upon our entrance to the dealership a heavily cologned, sport-coat garbed stud will hone in on the "weaker sex" first. Biff, looking every bit the former high school jock turned salesman, will then take her by the arm to the hottest little coupe on the floor. My love and I exchange glances to confirm that she, in this case, will play the "good cop."

After allowing him to show us all of the latest innovations in the auto industry (as if we have been living on Mars for the last ten years), Elise would then hit him with that for which we are actually shopping – something "wholesome," in which we can safely cart around our SIX CHILDREN.

At this point, all discussion of sun-roofs, semi-hemis, mag wheels and leather upholstery comes to a screeching halt. Several compliments about her looking much too young to have so many children provide the perfect segue for his next act. Setting aside moves more appropriate for a high school dance floor, our new friend becomes *The Price Is Right*'s Bob Barker. We stroll toward the larger SUVs and the highlighted features become the roominess and extra cup holders available in the grander, very "family friendly" vehicles.

As he continues to direct his comments to the "little woman," I remain the strong silent type. Several times will I saunter over to the little sports model and look longingly at the engine – though I would not know an overhead cam from the windshield washer fluid reservoir.

Stopping just short of asking to see pictures of the "little ones," the conversation invariably turns toward what extras she might like to have to enhance their safety and riding pleasure (as well as his commission). Extra horsepower for needed acceleration, crushed velour seats, and satellite mapping systems roll off his tongue like one of my orders at *McDonald's*. But these are countered by Elise with concerns about sufficient leg room for those horses we call sons and a CD player with controls in the back, her concession to the kids to keep me from tuning in to sports talk shows on the radio!

Sensing that we might not be the buyers that will enable him to become "salesman of the month," the conversation rapidly turns to dollars and cents and the various packages that might fit within our budget – something we have yet to mention. Once again, I stroll away from the desk, leaving my helpless little waif to flip through all of the options.

Of course, everything being way too expensive for us, Elise explains, "Though we would love to have each and every feature you mentioned, we just cannot afford it." Upon revealing the budget that the "old fuddy-dud" (aka husband, aka CFO) has set aside for the purchase, the salesman is crestfallen. He will swear that there is no way he can meet that price. At which point, she thanks him for his time and beckons me to join her as she heads for the door.

More often than not, the car salesman extra-ordinaire will jump up from his chair to stop us from leaving and ask if we are planning to trade in our old car. If not, he might be able to "do something with the price" on some vehicle to fall within our price range.

Coaxing us back to his desk, he pulls out a three ring binder with all of the cars that he has in inventory. Flipping pages like crazy, he exclaims, "Yes, something can be found within your price range – if you are content with basic black and a small engine.

However, if you are willing to go up just a bit in price, I happen to have something else on the lot..."

And, at that point, we take the infamous trip out to the parking lot to look at a fleet of what appears to be homogenous cars, all sweltering in the summer heat with little plastic bras covering their front ends. Lacking the physical attributes normally associated with those pieces of lingerie, I assume they are to avoid damage from the gravel churned up by customers as they "kick the tires."

During this round of negotiation, the "good cop" will find the vehicle that we came to buy in the first place and suddenly fall in love with it. Beaming like a new college graduate, the salesman will then take her by the arm and lead her back to his desk to discuss how he might be able to get to a mutually agreeable price on such a car. Following in their wake, as "bad cop" I casually kick gravel onto several cars, not willing to risk injury to my foot by kicking any tires!

Once settled back in his comfort zone, Biff pulls out that exotic tool of every car salesman – the small, handheld calculator. These LED-faced anachronisms can now only be found in car dealerships and cereal boxes! Punching on keys that are way too small for his finger, he copiously jots down several resultant sets of figures on the legal pad which has suddenly appeared on his desk. A bottom line number is developed.

Never verbalizing the amount, he slides the pad across the desk, reminding her, "That, of course, does not include taxes, registration fees, and dealer prep." (Is that last item the charge to move the vehicle from the lot to the front of the building? Or is it the cost of having the car's brassiere removed?)

The "good cop" appears ready to agree to such a figure though it is well above our budget but then retracts her concurrence as she acknowledges my scowling "bad cop" face. At long last, I receive some attention. I suggest, in a carefully rehearsed manner, that we continue to look elsewhere. Being my one line, I work hard at bringing it off with a certain degree of panache.

"But wait!" our little friend responds. "Perhaps, if you are really interested in purchasing a car today..." (Does anyone shop for cars without the intention to buy? Is the scent of the showroom really that alluring?) "If so, I will talk to the manager about doing something better on the price." Demonstrably placating me with a gentle hand to my knee, the "good cop" then graciously offers to entertain any improved pricing.

Typically, there will be several of these trips to the manager's office. Where does the manager sit, anyway? And why does he not just come out and talk to us directly?

(On one such shopping trip, the sales guy, having been gone for an abnormally long time, came back with what appeared to be mayonnaise on his lower lip! I kid you not. The idiot must have grabbed a sandwich, while "consulting with his manager." Needless to say, that session ended without a sale.)

After several more such trips to consult with the manager, each time offering a bit more in options, or a slight reduction in price, the "bad cop" finally grudgingly agrees on a price and we purchase the car. Elise has assured me that giving birth is less of a hassle.

And thus, previous car purchases have been concluded.

But now that I have a bit of time on my hands, I offered to handle this latest acquisition single-handedly. Though she may have enjoyed the result of previous such excursions, she hated wasting so much of our time. Thus, I would step up to shouldering this latest burden. I would do all of the research and shopping, and Elise could just revel in the end product.

For the next several days, I surfed the Internet seeking the latest, most efficient way to buy a car. Having perused several "Ten steps to buying a new car at the lowest possible price" sites, I was about to conclude that none were better than our process. All I needed was someone to step in for Elise to play Cop #2. But then, I stumbled upon "buying services."

For those unfamiliar, these are groups of retailers who are willing to provide various appliances, services, or cars at prices just slightly above their cost. They're willing to forego higher profit margins in the interest of increased volume – or so the banner at the top of one of their pages explained. You merely have to provide a host of personal information to obtain a membership, in some cases including the names and ages of each of your children. In return, they will then provide local dealers and a "secret code" to be divulged upon entering the establishment. After numerous comparisons, I selected two that promised me the car of my choice at a mere two hundred dollars over the dealer's cost!

Armed with my cryptic code bearing certificates I ventured out to visit several dealerships last Monday. Determined that I would make this a stress-free venture, I chose to approach this in a business-like manner. Eliminating all emotion, I would merely indicate what model I was looking for, including the specific options – right down to the color, and ask their price. I was confident that at minimum I would find a van for less than or equal to two hundred bucks over the cost shown on the Internet.

Mondays must be a slow day for car dealerships, for I was the only visible customer at each of the four I visited. Indeed, after three hours of shopping, including the use of my buying service certificates and a short stop for coffee and a donut, I had obtained two offers within fifty bucks of each other (only one of which belonged to an aforementioned buying service!). These were significantly below the other two dealers' "best" offers, though nowhere near the level I had computed from my earlier research on cost. Of course, the various options on each available vehicle made an exact comparison impossible.

A second visit to each of the dealers with the lowest price and I was finally able to negotiate a set of add-ons nearly equivalent to those we were seeking without an explosion of price. The last meeting was concluded with a handshake and a promise to return on Tuesday with my wife, a convenient delaying tactic on my part, to "close the deal."

Beaming with my latest achievement, I returned home to tell the love of my life about the great bargain I had obtained. Another previously shared responsibility had been shouldered by yours truly and saved both of us a lot of wasted time. There really is some value in being semi-retired.

Unfortunately, on Tuesday morning "the boss" had a consulting job, so I had to postpone our return to sign the papers until that afternoon.

As she left for her job my love mentioned that she might stop at a dealership that was near her client's office. Equipped with the details of my deal, including the outstanding price, she confirmed that we would visit "my guy" later that day to finalize the purchase.

Yep, you guessed it. Four hours later I received a call that sounded like it was being made from a phone booth. It was my own little "Agent 007" doing her best imitation of a spy in a grade B movie. She was at a dealership that I had not visited and had bargained a deal for a more luxurious model van, with additional features, at a price that was five hundred bucks cheaper than what I had gotten! I was so appalled that my first reaction was to reject the deal. After all, I had my pride to think of...

That lasted about twenty seconds. She then reminded me of the added savings and the fact that this van had seats that hid away in the floor versus being dragged out of the car when not needed. The recollection of pains in my lower back reminded me how much I hated that latter feature and sealed the deal.

Reminding myself that "pride goeth before the fall," I signed off, giving her the green light to conclude the deal. I would call my guy to tell him of our decision to keep the old car for another year or so (a little white lie – after all, is a week not almost the equivalent of "or so"?).

So much for my negotiation skills, I will just have to take my career search in another direction.

Hmm, there was that note tacked up at the bagel shop - a group of senior citizens is seeking someone to transport them. Let me see, if I take seven at a time...

Used Car Salesman

After several months of pursuing a second career via the Internet, career counseling, and trials by error, I have recently found my attention focused on the classifieds of our local newspaper. There are tons of job listings therein.

However, I was not looking at them as a vehicle to answer the fulfillment of my passion; though there are plenty of ads that suggest that those submitting the listings might be interested in doing so! Rather, I was seeking a means of selling our old car. It felt like losing a member of the family!

Having been with us for a large number of years, I had grown quite attached to it. Sure, the AC may not have been working for the last couple years, but the power windows operated well. And I enjoy the breeze in my hair when on the open road. (Picture not the hot stud in the convertible with his tresses flowing in the wind, but rather the shaggy dog sticking his head out the window of the car next to him.) Unfortunately, other members of the family did not feel quite the same way about fresh, though a bit warm, air blowing in their faces. Thus, rather than pouring more money into my dying "friend," a new car was purchased. It was my duty to find a new home for the old boy.

Some folks trade in an old car when purchasing a new one. Indeed, that is what we did prior to being "educated" by Jack, an old timer who used to live down the block. He had three Saabs, all in various states of disassembly, parked in front of his house thus labeling him as an auto expert.

Shortly after we moved here some thirty years ago, Jack found that we were shopping for a new car. He inquired as to what we were going to do with the old one. I thought for sure he wanted to add it to his armada of cars, most of which were in the midst of repair. When I told him I was going to trade it in, he laughed and insisted that I was naïve in the working of the used car industry. (I didn't even realize that there was such a thing!)

Jack insisted that if I placed an ad in the newspaper and, more importantly, in those little weekly fliers that are delivered unsolicited to our homes, I could easily get more money than any car dealership would offer. It would merely take a little patience, a bit of backbone and some astute bargaining power – none of which was I confident that I possessed.

Well, I did as he suggested, and must admit that we succeeded in selling the car for several hundred dollars more than a dealer had proffered on a trade-in. Being actively employed at the time, I failed to consider seriously pursuing "flipping cars" as a potential alternative career. However, now that I am "between positions," if you will, I may have to look back upon that experience as an internship. In light of that, and subsequent similar successful sales, I viewed this latest sale of our van as a means of testing these waters as those of a potential career...

And so I found myself perusing the classifieds. The process of posting an ad involves so much more than just calling the paper. Try to describe in thirty words or less – the standard allowance for a basic listing in the newspaper's used car ads, the automotive "love of your life."

The sticker that was attached to the car when it sat in its pristine beauty on the dealer's lot over a decade ago consisted of hundreds of words and numbers. The ad had to encompass the standard information – model, size of engine, power features, color, and asking price. My reduced "sticker" had to attract potential buyers with all of the extras that my little gem possessed. I had to let them know that it has an air conditioner (though not fully operational), radio (that picks up most, but not all, stations), nearly spotless interior (stained from when my oldest son, Jared, lost his lunch on that trip to Gram's), and other attractive options. Not exactly being a man of few words this was a daunting task.

After writing out several drafts, while poring over the latest, the love of my life intervened. "Give it to me. You'll never get it done."

A quick five minutes of scribbling and she handed it back to me. "Here, I put the required details together, now just call the paper and list the car. It's not supposed to be the Great American Novel!"

Convinced that it would not attract any interest, I reluctantly called in the bland thirty words. I agreed to pay to have it listed for two weeks though I was positive that if I had been allowed one more shot at a draft we would not have needed more than a single weekend.

The next step was preparation of the vehicle for inspection by potential buyers. A simple wash and vacuuming just wouldn't suffice. Rather, I had to make this ten-year-old clunker look like something that should be in a new car showroom.

So, in addition to the normal cleansing (not done frequently over the last few years), out came the little bottle of touch-up paint that the dealer provided when we first purchased the car. It has sat, unopened, in the glove compartment ever since. I dabbed a bit on the various little dings and scratches to eliminate the obvious rust spots. The subsequently shiny spots, contrasting with the faded finish, were not much of an improvement.

Making these cosmetic changes, I regretted the decision to not have that dent in the rear fender addressed two years ago when some dope backed into me in the mall parking lot. Alas, I will just stand in front of it when showing the car.

While cleaning the windows I found that the state vehicle inspection had expired two months earlier. Drat!! Now I had to have it inspected prior to the sale – another fifty bucks down the drain. Fortunately, being "semi-retired" I could get it done in sufficient time to still have the car available for sale on the upcoming weekend.

Unfortunately, the inspection process is more than a review to ensure that all of the lights are working. I was told that the car needed two new tires to pass. (Oh boy, this was not going to go over well with "the boss" who wanted me to sell the car long before the inspection expired!) A quick trip to a wholesale tire store, in which I pleaded for the cheapest tires available, and I was set back another couple hundred bucks – vans take large tires!

The two new tires now made the others look really old. Since most used car buyers like to "kick the tires," though I have no idea what that proves, I decided I had to do something about them.

A visit to the auto parts store and I bought some magic liquid that supposedly makes old tires look like new. (In retrospect, black shoe polish would have done the same and been a lot cheaper.) While there, I also bought a hubcap to replace the one that had fallen off some time last winter. But, since that would make the others look old, I had to buy some other magic liquid to make the other caps sparkle as well. Another fifty bucks down the tubes. I was beginning to wonder if I could sell the car for enough to cover all of these little improvements!

Now that the car shined like a "new" hundred-and-twenty-thousand mile-car, I turned my attention to its interior. Not content with the little car vacuum that one of the kids bought me one Father's Day, I pulled out the huge wet/dry vac from the garage. Intent on removing every last pebble and French fry, I inadvertently sucked up the carpeting – oh boy, that can't be good. Well, a little glue and it should be just fine. I then crawled under each seat, finding numerous straws and gum wrappers, as well as plenty of coins – hey, maybe they would cover the cost of the hubcap!

Next was the removal of a decade of dust and dirt from the windows, seats and dashboard. While a lot of elbow grease seemed to do the trick, no matter how hard I scrubbed the steering wheel there was no way that grime would come off. I finally resigned myself to leaving it with the thought, "It gives the car character."

I was confident that my old friend was now ready for the hordes that would be descending upon him once the ads appeared in that Friday's paper.

Now focusing on the sale, I recalled the importance of removing the registration sticker from the front windshield once the sale takes place. Failing to do so, the car would be traced back to me if the new owners do not properly register it.

That is exactly what happened several years ago, when we sold a small car to a couple of shady characters who paid in cash. Anxious to complete the sale, and not interested in doing any further business with them, I took their payment in several large bills and never got their names or addresses.

Three days later we got a call from the State Police asking if we were still the owners of that particular car. My first thought was that I had not filed the proper sales taxes on the sale and they were now after me! After explaining that we had sold it the prior weekend, we were told it had been used in a bank robbery!

The car, they continued, had been abandoned without plates. (I had known enough to take them off – I could get money back from the state when I surrendered them.) The police had tracked me down from the registration sticker which was still on the vehicle.

Accepting my claim of innocence and a precise description of the buyers – "Two huge guys with Caribbean accents" – they thanked me for my cooperation and warned me to remove the sticker on any future sales. (Since then, when selling a car I get the name, address, and phone number, as well as the names of all children and pets, of the buyer!)

Well, our latest ad was surprisingly effective – we had two potential buyers come to view the car the second day it appeared. The first guy arrived in late morning.

My initial step was to establish a "personal" relationship with my "client." After introductions, I asked what he did for a living (disguised method of checking his credit, though I will ultimately insist that he pay with cash).

Big mistake. The potential buyer spent more time discussing his new appliance store than checking out the car! He kept telling me of the wonderful discounts he could offer me. (I began to wonder if his offer would include a new washer and dryer.) Finally, he made a bid that was significantly below my asking price.

Directing his attention to the new tires, I made a counter-offer. But all he did was resume the recitation of the wonderful appliances at his store. He did not make a counter-counter-offer before leaving. However, he did call four days later to repeat his original offer and asked if I was yet interested. Refusing to accept his price I fully expected him to call again the following week.

Later that same day, two burly fellows came to look at the car. Not so much into conversation, they were more aggressive in examining the car. Not only did they kick the tires, but after having me start the engine they asked me to "pop the hood" to allow them to see the engine.

I readily reached under the dashboard to release the hood latch and came around the front of the car to open it. However, the hood was not so accommodating. I could not get the stupid latch to let go.

With them looking on, I returned to the release under the dashboard. Pulling so hard I was afraid it would break, one of the gents moved toward the hood and reached beneath it. To my relief, he was able to open it and we all then stood around admiring the "smoothly" idling engine. (For the life of me, beyond confirming that the engine was there, I have no idea what people are looking at when they do this).

After several "hmms" and "ahas," they closed the hood and stepped away. Thanking me for the opportunity to see the car, they told me that they had a few other cars to look at and left, promising that they would be back.

I am still awaiting their call.

Not a single call came in during the next two weeks the ad appeared in the papers. Hmm, wonder what the dealer would have offered on a trade-in. I began to question whether I had the stomach to pursue a career in the used car industry. Wish I knew if Jack, who moved off the block some ten years ago, might be interested in buying the car for its parts?

But, as any good salesman would tell you, the key to success is good marketing. Since my love's classified listing was not producing much traffic I decided to pursue another technique. I placed a *FOR SALE* sign in the front windshield of the van and parked it on a relatively busy street just a short distance from our home. This was taking a real risk, since the car no longer had plates. But hey, "One must take risk to realize the rewards" – a direct quote from Investing in the Stock Market 101.

Within two days, I got a call about the car!

However, it was not one inquiring about the price. No, rather it was the police – the car had been involved in an accident!

Yes, a car had gone through a stop sign at the adjacent corner, hitting another car which then crashed into the rear of my van! Thankfully, no one was hurt, but the bumper of my van was now resting on the ground beneath a badly dented tailgate. Guess this will delay the sale a bit longer.

But even this has a bright side. I have become well acquainted with the world of insurance claim adjusters – perhaps a possible career path?

The car has again taken up residence in my driveway for the last week and has yet to be repaired. But I have not given up; I am still pursuing the sale of the car – even in its damaged state. It will be a true test of my salesmanship.

Ah, have to run. The phone is ringing. Perhaps someone is answering our earlier ad. If so, they will be pleased to see just how "negotiable" my price is!

Civic Duty

A few months ago I got a call from my eldest son, Jared. The Libertarian in the family, he is suspicious of all things related to the government. Well, he was calling to complain that he had gotten that letter in the mail that so many of our society dread – a summons to jury duty.

"I don't have time for that nonsense. I will have to get off from work – and I don't think they'll pay me while I'm serving my time! What a waste.

"Why, with my luck, I'll get stuck on some long-term Grand Jury." And so went most of the rest of his continuing rant, leaving little room for my comforting words of wisdom.

After hanging up, my mind began to wander. Thoughts of pursuing a career in the legal world began to swirl through my head. Perhaps something intimately involved in our country's system of jurisprudence.

No, I am not thinking of returning to Law School – I've spent enough time in classrooms over the years. And, though I think I would look good in judicial robes, I am sure you need some legal experience or degree to get one of those jobs. And, no, I am not joining the Police Auxiliary Force – blue is not a good color on me and what good is that uniform if you don't have a gun to go along with it?

Nahh, instead I'm thinking of something else in the courtroom – a juror. I am well-qualified, and now have plenty of time. Indeed, it is something that has eluded me over the years, though I cannot understand why.

I have voted in every major election for the past thirty years or so.

I've been a resident of this state for all my life and a county resident for more than three decades!

Can't be due to the presence of a criminal record, I can confidently state that mine is completely clean. Never have I committed a felony. Why, I've not even contested a single traffic ticket; even though those bestowed were done so erroneously – probably due to faulty radar guns. Heck, last week I returned a printer that my partner had purchased for one of her clients. Though it had been a tax exempt purchase the sales clerk inadvertently included the associated sales tax in the refund which I did not discover until I was on my way home. Well, just like ol' honest Abe Lincoln, I returned to the store and had the refund adjusted.

The bottom line is that I am an honest, law-abiding citizen.

WHY, THEN, IS IT SO DIFFICULT FOR ME TO GET CALLED FOR JURY DUTY?

The love of my life has been summoned at least twice over the last ten years. My children who have moved away have each had to submit proof of their change of residence to be exempted from serving. Tara actually received a summons to appear while residing in the South Pacific in the midst of a two year assignment in the Peace Corps!

Yet I have not gotten a single note from our Commissioner of Jurors.

Perhaps the government has lost track of me. I am not on the public dole. I do not receive a federal pension. I don't collect Social Security. Perhaps I should withhold my tax payments! Of course, with my lack of a steady income would they even notice?

The fact is, I am more than qualified to fill the position of juror. I have watched every episode of *Law and Order*, some of them twice – not remembering the episode until the DA pulls the rabbit out of the hat in his closing argument.

Such shows have been a staple of my entertainment diet for years. I have been known to emulate Denny Crane, the lead name of the firm featured in *Boston Legal*. It has been said that I resemble Daniel J. Travanti, the District Attorney in *Hill Street Blues*. (Now that I think of it, he was the police chief, not the DA, but I did want to slip in that resemblance thing, though the love of my life might dispute it.)

Why, my clarity of thought and ability to see through conniving liars has been compared to the most famous legal mind of all – Perry Mason. My love has noted that, while digesting those "free vacation" offers that come in the mail, I've shown the same legal acumen as E. G. Marshall of that sixties TV show, *The Defenders*.

(Side bar: Perhaps it wasn't Travanti in *Hill Street Blues* but Karl Malden in *The Streets of San Francisco*. Hmm, must be the distinguished look that triggered the comparison.)

Who better to serve on a jury?

Who is better equipped to wade through the myriad constitutional, ethical, and often scientific issues to be weighed by a jury in their effort to render a well-thought-out and appropriate verdict? I have the education, the moral fiber, and the religious upbringing; some might say I've been preparing for the role of juror for several years.

While others may have watched similar shows on TV and at the cinema, few have focused on the behaviors of the juries as I have. I can even describe the wardrobe of each of the male jurors on the last twelve episodes of *Ally McBeal*. (Not an easy feat since, like most men, the camera tended to focus primarily on the short skirts and spiked heels of the leggy female attorneys.)

I have even made note of the change in the fashions of the male jurors. Though the attorney's ties may have gone from dull solids and stripes to the more fashionable florals and paisleys, they still wear suits. Rare, however, is the tie that is seen in today's jury box. The suits and sports coats of the sixties (the latter usually connoting a blue collar juror) have evolved to the more casual dress made popular in Corporate America in the nineties.

What must I do to get the attention of the powers that decide who will and who will not serve on jury duty? The aforementioned summons to my son was the second or third such beckoning for someone who had not yet voted in his third presidential election! Where was the equity of the system?

And, as if to rub salt into my wounds, Jared indicated that he would pursue a postponement due to vacation plans he had made! I cannot get summoned and he is seeking to avoid the opportunity. I was incensed!

Over dinner that evening I may have voiced my frustration and, as is so often the case, the love of my life came up with a solution. "Why don't you just contact them and volunteer to serve? I'm sure they will accept your offer."

She continued, "When I went online to explore the postponement process for Jared, I think I saw some means for volunteering for jury duty. You should look into it."

And so it was, without further prompting, that the following day I pursued such a possibility. Hopping on the Internet, I did my own homework on the staffing of juries. I found that she was, in fact, correct. I could apply online for the opportunity to serve on a trial of my peers.

The questionnaire was quite intense. I had to certify that I could communicate in English – ducked a fastball there, thankfully the questionnaire was not in Swahili!

They asked for my current address and county of residence. Several lines later they asked if I was a resident of the county listed above. Fearing another curveball, I thought long about the difference between "county of residence" and having an abode in such county. Which would make you a resident? Hmm, wonder who they would be trying that they were seeking a set of peers of such great intellectual acuity? I marked "yes."

The next question asked if I was over the age of eighteen. Has volunteering for jury duty become a fad amongst teenagers? Is this the latest way to get out of going to class? Who would have thought that completing the request for date of birth at the top of the form would have negated the need for this question? Of course, those reading this application are expert in the legal profession – not necessarily known for their mathematical talents.

They next asked if I have been convicted of a felony. And if so, I was to provide a description of the crime, the court that heard my case, and the date of its occurrence – all of which was to fit on the following single line. Heck, I could not fit the details about my wife's latest speeding ticket on one line! How was some guy supposed to describe an armed robbery that took place in Queens fourteen years ago while he was high on drugs and his girlfriend was sitting in the stolen getaway car, pregnant with their illegitimate child?

And, besides, I thought convicted felons lost their rights as citizens. I am pretty sure they cannot vote; yet, they can sit in judgment of their peers? Do you see any irony there? Hmm, so they cannot vote for some sleazy politician to take office but can hear his case once he is caught doing something illegal. Makes sense on some level I am sure...

After several other pages of more mundane information – have you served on a jury in the last four years, do you harbor any ill feelings toward any law enforcement agency, do you have any dietary preferences in the event that your jury is sequestered, and so forth – I was ready to transmit my request to the powers that be. One hit of the ENTER button on my keyboard and I would be in the system. Oh, the thought of it still sends shivers up and down my spine. To think – I would now be a member of that group of society that Jerry Ohrbach often referenced when he said that some "perp" had been "in and out of the system for years!"

Yes, I did it. I submitted my request. At long last, I was officially "in the system."

But then, I had little evidence of my solicitation, other than the locally printed copy. My fate had been cast to the ether of the Internet. For weeks I held my breath in anticipation of their response. (Well, not really held my breath, but you get the idea...)

Then, a few days ago I got that magical package in the mail. In what was little more than a four-fold forty-weight paper stock, my eyes landed on that which was printed on a red stripe above my address – **IMPORTANT**: *Jury Summons Enclosed*. (Actually, that was misleading, there was no enclosure. The entire summons is written on the four folded postcard-like pages.)

Yes, I was to be a juror!

What type? Federal? State? Perhaps Grand Jury?

As I ripped it open, I found the words with the answer. It read: *You are hereby summoned to serve as a ** TELEPHONE STANDBY JUROR **.* I was crestfallen.

Since when do they do "call in" trials? Would the judge, plaintiffs, defendants, and all of the jurors be brought together via conference call? What about the oak paneled trial room? The jury box? The hours of deliberations, and possible sequestering with fully paid hotel room and meals? My opportunity to impress the guy in robes with my reading from that infamous piece of paper – "We, the jury, find the defendant..."?

Dismally, I regained my composure and read further.

It was a County Juror Summons. I was to report to the Supreme Court Building in our county's seat. My head began to swim again. Was I being beckoned to hear local traffic violations or was I being asked to sit on the highest court of the land?

I reread "Supreme Court" several times. I always thought those guys met in Washington, D.C. But then I recalled seeing something about Circuit Judges traveling around to the various county seats in some of those old Westerns. Maybe the boys, oops, sorry Ruth Bader Ginsburg, make that the "guys," would be hitting our county in their travels?

Aw, just kidding. As I continued to read I found that it was indeed a New York State Court. But still, I would be a juror! Or so I hoped.

Why, might I suggest that I would be an excellent foreman? Indeed, I would have done a much better job of managing those *Twelve Angry Men* than Martin Balsam did in that famous cinematic courtroom drama. Rather than focusing solely on the thorny issues of the case, I would have drawn the attention of the group to the delectable donuts and plentiful sandwiches that were provided by the Justice Department. How outraged could they have remained if they had partaken of a good pastrami-on-rye with mustard and sauerkraut? Or perhaps a tasty BLT? Just the thought makes me salivate. And, who have you ever seen enraged while their mouth was watering over the thought of some tasty little dish? I rest my case. Put me in charge of a jury! Where do I sign? Or should I say, volunteer?

I continued to read. The document was the size and weight of four postcards – without the pictures. It explained that only a select number of potential jurors would have to report each day. I was assigned a number and beginning the evening preceding the first date of my term of service, I was to call an 800 number to see if my number fell within the range provided by a recorded message. If so, I was to appear the following day. Yesterday was the first day I could call...

My number was well beyond the range of those called for today. I am irate! If I don't get to serve I will go into total despair!

As directed, I will call again tonight.

For now I must go. I have three episodes of *Law and Order* on DVD to watch. After that I must think about what I will wear if called. Something that will get me noticed – perhaps a Hawaiian shirt? Can't be too many of those in the jury pool, after all, it is after Labor Day!

Juror

Yesterday began in a bright and glorious fashion. After a long period of hope and frustration, my initial day of jury duty had finally arrived! Yes, the prior evening I had called and found that my jury summons number was within the range of those being gathered the following day. In celebration of the call I took the love of my life out for dinner with some dear friends. Indeed, I was treated with more than usual respect – perhaps the result of my regaling them with some of the heroic events I anticipated of my upcoming term as JUROR. This could be the first step toward a productive career in the legal profession.

As I laid out my wardrobe for the day, I still had not overcome my anxiety about the proper attire for my new position. Deeming a suit too formal (did not want to be mistaken for one of the attorneys) I considered a sport coat and tie. But then, recalling that, statistically, most criminals come from the lower socio-economic levels of our society (any full season of *Law and Order* will bear out this fact), I felt that a tie would distance me from the defendant. It got tossed. Next was the question of a button-down or golf shirt. Not wanting to alienate the straight and narrow prosecution team, I elected to go with a white... golf shirt. Of course, since it might be chilly in the courtroom, and still wanting to separate myself from the others to warrant consideration as jury foreman, I opted for a muted hounds-tooth sport coat – stylish, but not over the top.

Driving to the Supreme Court Building my mind raced with thoughts of what was about to happen. I ran through the whole *voir dire* process. For those not familiar, that is where potential jurors are asked background questions, the answers for which may provide cause for exclusion from sitting on the jury. For more details see *Matlock*, Episode 7, 1993 season. Hmm, how would I get in the fact that I had successfully managed diverse groups of people for most of my thirty-year career? Uh, make that *financial* career – in the event it is a civil case and they need someone on the jury to compute an appropriately-sized financial settlement. Drat, I should have brought along a small pocket calculator...

Traffic was light and I arrived in the parking lot reserved for potential jurors fully fifteen minutes prior to my scheduled report time. However, upon entering the building, I was confronted with several lengthy lines of people waiting to pass through security! Finding one designated as being for potential jurors, I assumed my position at the end wondering how those failing to report on time would be treated.

Dutifully following the serpentine line around the rope-connected stanchions, the infamous X-ray tunnel finally was within reach. I turned to see that the line continued to snake back to the entrance which was now a good nine-iron shot away. It was comforting to know that I would not be the only juror to be late.

Next came what has become the standard greeting of official America. A fully armed and tough looking police officer shouted, "Place all bags, laptops, cell phones and other metal objects on the table. Empty your pockets of all keys and change, placing them into a bowl, before passing through." All said with a frown. Is *Walmart* the only place left where you actually get greeted with a smile?

I have a personal hatred of these screenings, but not necessarily for the reason that others may hate them. For me it is the fact that it calls attention to the fact that I am one of the 0.00036% of America that does not have a cell phone! Invariably, as I place my few coins and keys in the box, I am asked, "And your cell phone?"

Officer Krumpke did just as expected – and in front of the very same jury candidates I was hoping to lead as their foreman! Ugh. Thinking quickly (did I mention that I had already consumed three cups of coffee to ensure my being alert when called), I deftly replied, "Um, I know the drill. I left it at home." Then I smugly stepped through the detector.

But then, what little evidence of *savoir-faire* I may have exhibited was lost when I went to recoup my belongings – my change fell all over the floor! I think the car keys interrupted their smooth flow as I tipped the bowl into my outstretched hand.

Scooping them up off the floor (I must have left at least seventy five cents there), I abandoned those closest behind me and trotted to a door with the sign, *Jurors,* clearly displayed.

It opened onto an auditorium holding perhaps five hundred people. Aha, so these are my peers! Looking around for an empty seat (no easy task since it was obvious that a ton of other potential jurors knew about the long security lines), I spotted one near the front that would require my climbing over only four people.

At last, after a full fifteen minutes of staring at an empty podium, fearing that I had missed the opening remarks, a portly toupee-laden man bearing a name tag identifying him as Herman Potter assumed the position at the front of the room. Tapping the microphone the requisite three times and skipping any introduction, he began, "Please make sure you all have your summonses with you." I proudly took mine out of my pocket, only to hear him continue, with a silly little smirk, "If not, duplicates can be gotten from Millie, who's sitting up here at the front of the room."

In his most informal style he continued. "Now, none of us, including me, really want to be here on this sunny day. However, I'm here because I need the money – this is my job. You, on the other hand, have a civic duty to fulfill."

Not sure if this was meant to endear him to his audience, but his comments did not seem to bring smiles to anyone, though he was performing like Jay Leno. Some guy in the rear finally brought this nonsense to an end by yelling out that our humorist could not be heard!

Not the least bothered, Herman called back, "It doesn't matter, there's a film presentation about to begin that will cover everything you need to know. So just sit back and enjoy." He then left the podium. I am still not sure why he appeared in the first place.

We then sat through a twenty-minute video which opened with the classic "man on the street interviews." Those appearing were identified as "potential jurors." Each bemoaned the fact that their lives were disrupted to serve on a jury. "Why did this curse befall me?" "Couldn't someone else do it?" They all had more pressing matters.

Based on the murmurings of the crowd, it was apparent that the film was falling on receptive ears. All, that is, except for me! I wondered if I was the only civic-minded person in the room.

A severe-looking, elderly woman suddenly appeared on screen and proceeded to provide what sounded like an eighth grade social studies lecture on the importance of a trial by one's peers. She, who turned out to be the State's Chief Judge, then explained our state's entire judicial structure. We were to hear cases being held in the State's Supreme Court, which, despite its name, is only the third highest in the state. I would detail those above it here, but I dozed off during that part of the video.

Several catcalls from the audience roused me from my slumber. Not sure what had provoked them, but I noted that Judge Fitzmeyer, now appearing in full judicial robes, was providing a virtual tour of a populated courtroom, describing each character and their roles in a trial. I could almost smell the mahogany of the seats where the jurors would sit. Ooh, I could not wait.

The good Judge then wrapped up her presentation with heartfelt thanks that we had taken our civic duty to heart and were prepared to uphold the law of the land. The video ended with some stirring marching music and the American flag flapping nobly in the breeze – I expected to be told to stand and rattle off the Pledge of Allegiance!

Instead, as the screen went to black, another autocratic looking civil servant came to the podium. Identifying himself as the Commissioner of Jurors, he reaffirmed the "burden of serving." (What's with everyone here? They make it seem like we're participants in a new Ebola vaccine test!) I was ready to stand on my chair and tell him that I, for one, had volunteered to do my duty and was proud of it. (I am one to act spontaneously.) Fortunately, the fat lady next to me refused to hold my book as I struggled to get out of my seat, thus saving me from what might have been an embarrassing moment.

The commissioner droned on, "As you sit, numerous judges are convening sessions in courtrooms throughout the building. At the appropriate time, they will issue a request for a number of potential jurors. Someone will then return to this podium and call out a list of names. Those called are to convene at the front of the room and will then be led to the proper courtroom."

Most of his ramblings were silently accepted until he said, "Until called all should remain seated here, though brief visits to the adjacent canteen or restrooms are allowed." That brought several moans from the crowd.

Ignoring the feedback, he wrapped up his spiel with, "If it is necessary for you to return tomorrow, you don't have to report until ten o'clock, since you will not need to view the Judge's video again." I almost cheered at the suggestion that this assignment might indeed be multiple days! However, I noticed that I was the only one smiling at this point. God help any defendants who would have a jury selected from this somber group.

Almost as an afterthought, prior to stepping away, he directed us to pass our summonses to the end of the aisle. A set of civil servants suddenly swept out of nowhere like ushers taking up a collection in church.

The elderly woman standing at the end of our aisle held out her hand for the documents being passed to her. She addressed the young guy wearing shorts at the end of the row. "You know, a judge would find your outfit offensive. You might want to go home to change." His response was to ignore her and continue reading his newspaper! Boy, some people have no respect for authority.

Dropping the friendly motherly tone, she continued in a more official one. "If you get rejected for inappropriate clothing, you will not have met your juror requirement. You will receive another summons to appear." I could tell from his expression, or lack thereof, that the threat did not really put the fear of God in him. Wanting to assist her in conveying her message, I tried to catch her eye to display my carefully thought out attire, nearly bursting the buttons on my sport coat in the process...

She never looked up. Instead she just proceeded to the next row to pick up another batch of summonses.

As I looked around, I saw that several folks had shown up not only in shorts, but also in jeans and tank tops and other "very casual" dress. All in direct violation of what was clearly printed on the back of our summons: *Proper attire required at all times: no jeans, shorts, tank tops, etcetera.* But was this addressed from the podium? No...

Resigning myself to the old adage, "the wheels of justice turn slowly" (or something like that), I settled in to read my book. Fortunately, I was just beginning a new one. The book I had just finished might not have been appropriate. Entitled *Judge and Jury*, it revolved around a mob boss' ability to prevent a successful trial by intimidating both the presiding judge and jury.

Just as I cracked open my newest read, the robust woman to my left decided to strike up a conversation. She proceeded to tell me that she was, "totally inconvenienced to be here." She had to take the day off from her job in some factory in Brooklyn, and she wasn't sure if she would get paid while she was here.

I weighed the idea of explaining that her employer had to pay her at least the forty bucks that the State would pay those of us who are unemployed. Hadn't she been watching the earlier video? But then, I really did not want to get into a lengthy exchange with her, so I merely nodded.

She went on to tell me she had three kids, two of whom had had run-ins with the law, "Though the amounts of drugs were small." She insisted that our entire justice system would be better served if they went after the "big fish" instead of the users...

Presuming I was listening, she then asked if I thought that her mentioning her kids might get her excused. I gave the same nodded response as before, though she failed to get my hint. Ten minutes later, she finished her one-sided conversation.

At eleven, they finally began calling out names. Each time, I sat up in my seat waiting to hear mine. But it was not to be so in the first, or the second, or the third group. I began to despair.

Another fifteen minutes of silence and they resumed calling names. My hefty neighbor was in this latest mix, though I did not catch her name. She stood with a huff, gathered herself (there was a lot to gather) and stormed off, seemingly upset that I was still sitting there. Little did she know that I was just as frustrated to have not yet been beckoned! Did they not see my sport coat?

A full half-hour later she returned. Plowing past me, she bent over explaining, "I lost my earring, did you happen to see it?"

Standing, for fear she would fall back on me, she found that for which she was searching. Then turning to me she took the opportunity to share, what was for her, bad news. "I got stuck on some jury! They told us all to go to lunch and be back by two!

"Then they're gonna put us all in vans and take us to the Criminal Court building for some trial!" She was spitting mad – but not more than me. I was tempted to offer to be her stand-in, but I noticed a newly acquired badge hanging from her neck that read "Gladys something or other."

I wished her luck, withholding the urge to tell her to just relate her opinions of the justice system as a means of getting excused. She then squeezed past me to exit the aisle. As she did so, I could have sworn she had a twelve-inch *Subway* sandwich sticking out of her bag.

As the clock neared noon, another group was called and my name rang out with a clarity that even I could not miss. I had dodged the bullet, for in the auditorium there could not have been more than a hundred or so prospective jurors left. At last, I was being called.

As directed, I followed my fellow jurors to Room Number Three. Ah, would this be my home for the next several days? Might we be sequestered here? Should I get a specific location so I could have my mail forwarded?

Alas, it was just a large room with rows of folding metal chairs. No jury box, no podium for the judge, no oak paneling. With an old fashioned blackboard on one wall, it looked more like a classroom than a courtroom.

After the forty or so of us were "comfortably" seated, good old Herman entered. In a very formal manner, he closed the door and then turned to address the group.

"A judge requested ninety jurors earlier for a criminal case to be held today." (My heart jumped at the words, CRIMINAL CASE.) "But they have entered a plea, so that group of jurors will be excused." (Perhaps Gladys had lucked out.)

"Another series of civil trials were supposed to be tried today," he continued, and my stomach started to sour at the past tense being used, "but they too have settled.

"Thus, our need for a jury pool is well below the number asked to appear today." I felt the bile rise in my throat.

"As such, you are all excused. No need to return. You all have an exemption from State court jury duty for six years and for two years from Federal jury duty."

EXEMPTION?! Did he not know that I volunteered? He was wasting a perfectly good juror!

"As you leave, be sure to pick up your Proof of Service Certificate. You may need it to support your exemption down the road. Also, please exit through the hallway to the left when you leave this room. I don't want to upset the candidates still in the auditorium who are being kept in case of a need for jurors in trials that may commence this afternoon."

A chorus of cheers rose from the group. I was tempted to stand, as the "self-nominated" foreman of this group, and insist on a more appropriate decorum. Instead, I merely sat there stunned. As the others walked out, I noticed that two of them were even wearing jeans!

Being the last to leave, I stopped to speak with Herman, a presumably senior civil servant. "I hate to bother you, but I volunteered for jury duty. Unlike some of them," pointing to those exiting the room, "I'd be happy to serve on a jury. Perhaps I can just return to the auditorium on the outside chance that another jury might be convened."

Shaking his head, he explained, "No, that's not possible. Once your card is pulled, it cannot be reentered into the pool." How silly of me to think that I could have possibly "reentered the pool." If only he knew how I had labored to get myself invited in the first place!

"Okay, but about that exemption." I continued, "How soon can I volunteer again?"

"Two years. And then you can resubmit your candidacy."

"Two years?! Are you kidding? Didn't the Chief Judge say that a half-million people get called for jury duty each year? What are the chances they'll notice me coming in a bit early?

"Heck, they seem to have lost my name for the last forty years, what are the chances that they'll have a record of the fact that I sat in the auditorium for a half-day in September?"

But Herman would not rise to my level of angst. Instead of continuing the discussion, he merely gathered his papers and turned to leave the room.

So much for my tour of duty as a Juror!! I tossed my Proof of Service Certificate into the first trash can I came upon in the hallway.

Fortunately, I am not easily deterred from that for which I have a passion. Refusing to accept my fate, my application for consideration for Jury Duty went out over the Internet last night. I had bookmarked the site when I first visited it several months ago.

Meanwhile, I must go and ensure that I am taping all of the new episodes of *Law and Order*. I would not want to miss out on any changes to proper trial procedures.

Breaking and Entering

The days are getting noticeably shorter. Though the temperatures have been unseasonably warm, the leaves have begun to change color and fall. We have turned the clocks back an hour. Yes, autumn is upon us and the dreaded winter is not far off. It is the time of "hunkering down." The air conditioners get put away, the screens come off the windows, and the seemingly endless raking of the yard begins!

This time of year tends to darken my spirits. No more refreshing laps in the pool. No more sitting at the beach enjoying a good book. The dying leaves and plants only contribute to my sullen mood.

Alas, I am not alone in these feelings. The evil side of the human spirit seems to awaken with the shortening of the days and the diminishment of visible plant life from all around us. The newspapers have reported that this time of year commonly brings an increase in criminal activity. As such, the police are on high alert and extremely sensitive to the observation of any "abnormal behavior."

Perhaps that is what led me to conclude, most recently, that I would never make it as a career criminal – specifically, one known for breaking and entering.

With the dropping temperatures, in-ground sprinkler systems must be drained lest the encroaching cold weather freeze the water-filled pipes. This is an annual chore that comes as regularly as Halloween.

The first few autumns after we had the irrigation system installed, I took time off from work to observe the ritual of shutting it down for the season as it was done by professionals. Subsequently concluding that I could do it for much less money, I have done it myself in each of the last several years.

The mere acquisition of an air compressor and I am on my way.

As such, one morning earlier this week, I went to the local tool rental agency and inquired about obtaining one. As usual, the guy behind the counter asked what size I wanted. Since I never recall which one I needed, I mumbled something like, "Enough to clear the water out of my sprinkler system."

Obviously not remembering me from previous visits, he asked for my phone number and, finding my file on his computer, quickly determined the model that I have been renting the last several years. After showing two forms of identification, having been through this numerous times I came prepared, he quoted me the cost to rent the compressor for four hours. He then told me he would have it brought out to my car.

Shortly thereafter, a young Charles Atlas approached the car in a stooped position, his posture only emphasizing the muscles in his huge back and shoulders. Wondering if he was rolling the compressor out from the store, I glanced around the car to see that the monster machine was indeed resting on what looked like a little red wagon – one without a handle. When he got to the car, he dismissed the boards I had brought to enable it to be rolled into the car. Instead, he just lifted the compressor and tossed it into the back of the van. Not to be outdone by this display of power, I pushed the button on my keychain and the hatch closed on the van. I left him standing in obvious awe and hopped into the car, moving quickly since the clock had begun ticking on my latest rental.

Now, draining the pipes, or "blowing out the lines" as they say in the trade, is really not rocket science. Turn off the source of water to the sprinklers; connect the air hose from the compressor to the water line leading out to the sprinklers; fire up the compressor, allowing it to build to its maximum pressure; and then flick another switch to allow the compressed air to escape into the hose, pushing the water out of the sprinklers at the distant end. It is the same principle that has gotten so many kids into trouble when given a drink with a straw.

After expelling whatever air it had accumulated in its tanks the compressor will sputter out. The process is then repeated until nothing but air is emerging from the sprinkler heads in each of the various zones.

Driving home, I was concerned about how I was to get the machine out of the car. In the past, one of my sons had always available to lend whatever muscle was necessary. But Adam was on a tour, Kyle was at school, and Jared was living in Vermont. Hmm – perhaps I could operate the compressor while it sat in the car, running a long extension cord to the nearest outlet. But then, the air hose that had to attach to the sprinkler line was only three feet long, so that idea died a quick death. I would just have to lug it to the junction at which the water enters the lines.

As in the past, I had promised to also blow out the sprinklers of my next door neighbor, Phil, and my sister-in-law, Celeste. I decided to stop at the latter's first, since Phil was not home and I had to get into his garage to operate the sprinkler controls.

Upon arriving at Celeste's house, I headed directly to the back door from where I would have access to the water valve controlling her sprinklers. But when I got there I found it was locked! She had promised to leave it open for me but had obviously forgotten I was coming on this day.

Fortunately, she had previously shown me where she kept a hidden house key. I made my way to the planter off her driveway, beneath which it was ensconced. Approaching it, I noticed a young guy that looked like a character from *West Side Story* – slicked back hair, white T-shirt, and tight black jeans. He was loitering at the curb in front of her house, which happens to be across the street from the local high school, so I assumed he was waiting for his girlfriend to come out. Watching "Rico" to be sure he was not looking my way, I furtively took the key from beneath the pot and returned to the back door.

Turning the key in the lock was not a problem. But as I opened the door, alarms began to blare like crazy! I then remembered that she had an alarm system – but I didn't know the code to disarm it!

Nevertheless, I rushed into the house and went straight to the alarm box. Frantically examining at it, I pushed the OFF button hoping for the best.

No such luck – the screaming alarms continued.

Eying a phone right next to the box, I attempted to call Celeste. The busy signal pulsing in my ear caused me to realize that the only number for her that I knew was her home number!

Assuming the alarm company would call her work or cell phone I bolted from the house and raced for home, where I had numbers for both. I could only hope to contact her first.

As I ran down the driveway I noticed my little friend, Rico, was staring at me from his car. The alarms were blasting outside the house as well as inside – she must have bought the "super, maximum security plan," but I had no time to stop and explain.

The usual five minute drive to my house took just over two minutes. After another two to find her number, I reached her, only to find that the alarm company had already called and the police were being dispatched.

When I explained what had happened, she agreed to call the alarm company and suggested that I not return for at least a half-hour. And, for when I did, she provided the password that was to be keyed in – MOTER, which had something to do with her kids' names.

Regaining my composure, in spite of hearing sirens for the next half-hour, I decided to spend the time blowing out my own sprinklers. Once again confronted with the infamous compressor in the back of the van, I had to come up with a way of getting it out of the car. With the rental clock ticking, I had no time for the construction of a go-kart to enable me to roll it out of the car. I would just have to lift it out on my own.

One good heave, an all too familiar burning sensation in my back, and I had it out and over the bumper, resting on the driveway. Thankful that it did not land on my foot, I lugged it to the rear of the house.

Turning off the main water valve, I spent the next hour alternately revving up the compressor and releasing its load of air into the selected zone of sprinklers. Once done, and finding that my neighbor was still not home I hoisted the stupid compressor back into the van and drove back to Celeste's.

Upon arriving, I noticed that my little friend had departed. Hmm, wonder if he was scared off by the cops. Or had he provided my description to them and then left for fear I might return?

Dismissing such thoughts, with the alarm code in hand I once again allowed myself into the house. Having set off the alarms, I headed straight to the box and set about punching in the code.

But those darn buttons are so small! I failed the first time, so I had to reenter the code. The third try was a success. At last, the screaming alarms ceased.

I could hear myself think.

I could also hear the phone ring!

Picking it up (doesn't everyone pick up calls in someone else's house?) I heard a voice announce that it was the alarm company. The young lady on the other end wanted to know the password.

Without thinking, yet always being a gentleman, I first introduced myself, including the fact that I was Celeste's brother-in-law. Since that did not seem to satisfy her, I then gave her the password. "MOTER, as in a car engine, except that the second O is really an E." I was so proud of myself for having the presence of mind to go through all that.

But, instead of being satisfied, she asked again for the password. As I was repeating myself, she said, "No, not what you key in, I need the *password*!"

Knowing nothing else, I repeated, "MOTER," after which she hung up. I assumed she was satisfied.

Returning to the car, I proceeded to once again strain my back lifting out the metallic beast and hauled it to the side of the house. Unlike the faucet at my house, her point of access was a standing pipe topped with a nut where the air hose would be attached. With the compressor revving itself up, I proceeded to remove the nut.

Unfortunately, in my haste, I had failed to first turn off the water at the main water valve.

You guessed it, water sprayed all over the place as the full pressure of the water line blew the wrench out of my hand. Unable to recap it, I left the spouting geyser and ran into the house to close the valve.

Dripping wet, I returned to the spot where I would be attaching the compressor to the sprinkler lines when I began to hear sirens. Oh no...

Sure enough, just as I turned on the now-properly connected compressor, I spied two of our county's finest running up the drive with hands on their holstered guns. They stopped in their tracks when they saw me.

Talk about intimidating! There they stood with what looked like ammo belts across their chests. They had on those funky leather leg wraps, just below the knees, making them look like they had just hopped off motorcycles! But no, these guys were from the real crime stopper squad. Their car, lights still flashing, sat blocking my van at the foot of the driveway. I was truly cornered.

But wait, I had no reason to run. I wasn't going to try to escape – but did they know that?

Not wanting to aggravate them, I casually stepped out from the yard and haltingly introduced myself. For the second time in fifteen minutes I was explaining my relationship to Celeste. "Uh, I'm the owner's brother," dropping "in-law" in the interest of speed, "I'm just here blowing out her sprinkler lines."

Guess the water dripping from my head was insufficient for them to believe my story, for they never removed their hands from their holsters. The bigger of the two demanded to see identification.

Slowly – I've watched enough cop shows on TV to know the procedure – I turned my back to them and reached into my back pocket to retrieve my wallet. Not that I was nervous, but the first thing I handed him was my Blood Bank Donor Card. When I realized my error, I hurriedly fished out my license.

In response to his question as to whose house it was, I told him and then he questioned why I had a different last name than "my sister!" Drat, I had to then go into the "in-law" part, though my mind was already working out how I was going to get the compressor back in time if they elected to "take me down to the station house."

At that point the compressor reached its max and suddenly stopped its racket.

The silence was deafening.

Perhaps they saw my knees shaking, for as quickly as they arrived, they seemed to buy my story and left. They didn't even ask to enter the house to ensure that any fellow thieves weren't ransacking it. (Think I have been watching too many crime shows on TV?)

I watched them pull away from the curb before returning to my labors. I could have really used a cup of coffee and a donut, or something stronger, at that point but who had time? I worked my way through the various zones, only to find, the hard way, that the last one was right next to where I had parked the compressor. Sure enough, as the air pushed the water out the sprinkler, yours truly was standing right over it! Ugh!

The ride back to my neighbor's was done wearing a soaked set of jeans. Compelled to get this done, I had promised Phil that I would do this chore for him, I looked at my watch and realized I was nearing my final hour of rental time. Pulling into the driveway, I saw that the love of my life had arrived home. As I was taking the compressor out of the van one more time (did I mention that I now walk with a stoop?), she came out to ask if I had had a problem with Celeste's alarm.

As I was about to provide all of the gory details, she held up her hand. "She's on the phone. Something about getting a third call from the alarm company?"

Leaving her in a confused state, I ran in to pick up the phone.

Celeste informed me that she had just gotten another call from the alarm company. Shocked about what must assuredly have been a mistake on their part, I went through each of the steps I had taken in the last hour. Being a bit sharper than I, Celeste deduced what had happened. It appears that I had left the door from her house to the garage open. Somehow, that had set off the alarm – guess I drove off faster than I thought, since I never heard it. More importantly, the police were on their way there once again!

I offered to return to the "scene of the crime," but she suggested I sit tight and allow them to do their check as they did the first time. I reassured her that I had locked the back door upon leaving. (Fortunately, I had not returned the key to its hiding spot, or I would have suspected that Rico had returned!)

Phil had by now returned home. Ignoring his question about my wet pants, I went right to his garage and began to blow out his lines. Of course, the whole time I was doing them, I heard sirens blaring in the distance. I took comfort knowing that the safety of the citizenry in our town is in good hands.

The compressor was returned within the allotted time. Julio, aka Charles Atlas, came out with his little red wagon and easily lifted the machine out of the car. As he rolled it back into the shop, I joked, "What, is it too heavy for you to carry it that short distance?"

At which point he turned toward me and, not muttering a word, flexed his muscles – revealing what I swear were "prison tats" on both of his arms. How did I miss them earlier?

And so it was that my morning of interaction with the long arm of the law came to an end. Having stopped for a cup of coffee and a nicely glazed donut, I returned to my office to continue my pursuit of the ideal second career. It will have to be one that is totally legit. I am just not cut out for a career of crime.

Meet and Greeter

My career search to date has pretty much focused on professions to which I have had previous exposure – either via observation or direct participation. But sometimes inspiration comes completely out of the blue. A recent trip to Atlantic City presented one of those occasions. It provided a glimpse of an occupation not previously considered.

No, not gambling.

Here is a clue. What do gigolos, politicians, and gerontologists all have in common?

A desire, or willingness, to "press the flesh" with the elderly.

So, you may ask, what is the function? The official title is "meet and greeter." Not heard of it? Well, me neither; that is, until my aforementioned trip. Allow me to back up a bit and explain how I came to be in New Jersey's famed gambling Mecca in the first place.

As I have mentioned my son, Adam, is an independent tour director who works with several travel companies. One such firm recently hired him to assist with an excursion they were sponsoring to Atlantic City. Upon returning he regaled us with stories of the excellent food and accommodations – they had even booked him a huge corner suite!

Now, though it is but a few hours drive, I have not visited that city, once more famous for its boardwalk, since it introduced gambling. As such, I

197

dropped a hint that I might like to join him on his next trip south. It might be fun to cruise the roulette and black jack tables together.

Well, my comment must have made it to one of the agency's owners, since I received a call earlier this month and was surprised to hear that they were seeking not Adam, but me! They wanted to know if I was interested in working a trip to Atlantic City for three days along with Adam and a few other tour directors. Being the professional that I am, and idly sitting in my office at the time, I mumbled, "Uh, sure..."

However, I had every intention of quizzing Adam about what would be involved and anticipated a subsequent return call, by me, stating, "Thanks, but no thanks."

Instead, over the following week, Adam convinced me that the "work" would be well within my skill sets. (Might they need someone to count the receipts, or develop a database of the guests' names, room numbers and total winnings/losses?)

Alas, with no good reason to refuse the offer, I finally elected to do it and just go with the flow. He did suggest that I make use of my extensive computer skills – "Make a name tag to wear. Identify yourself as part of the travel company's staff."

As such, a week ago Tuesday we left at the break of dawn to drive to the Atlantic City Hilton. Arriving an hour before the scheduled arrival of the guests, Adam introduced me to my new bosses – Carmella and Rosalie, the elderly owners of the Brooklyn-based travel company.

Carmella, garbed in a bright flowery blouse covering a substantial bosom and too tight ski pants, was the more outgoing of the two. Bedecked with blue hair, the color of which had obviously been poured out of a bottle, long dangling earrings and deep red lipstick, she looked more like someone you'd see at a Las Vegas roulette table. In greeting, she wrapped her huge arms around me and planted a big kiss on my cheek.

Rosalie, more subdued, was wearing a maroon velvet pants suit that may have been fashionable in the eighties. She took my hand in both of hers in greeting.

Passing on any further chit-chat, Rosalie soon thrust a bag of pins, a pile of envelopes and several pages of guest names at me. My first task was to ensure that each attendee had an envelope that held a gambling chit, luncheon coupon, and tickets to that evening's dinner show.

This was going to be a piece of cake.

After the remaining three members of the crew arrived I noticed that I was the only one wearing a self-made tag – four inches tall with one inch-inch letters printed at my desk at home. The others all had professionally imprinted metallic tags – of no more than a single inch tall. Great! Nothing like branding myself as the "newbie!"

Carmella brought us together to review the itinerary for the next two days. Subsequently to be shared with the guests, she also provided a few extra details that we were to communicate.

One of those items to be emphasized was an emergency number that could be dialed at any time of day or night from anywhere in the hotel. Looking around at what appeared to be a luxury hotel, not exactly a scene from *Survivor*, I wondered about the importance of this message. But, then, I was the rookie, who was I to question the pros?

Carmella continued her spiel. As each of fifteen buses arrived, a staff member (I assumed that now included me) would climb aboard, greet the visitors, and read the itinerary and special instructions to them. Then, after providing each with the aforementioned envelope and a copy of the itinerary, assist them in debarking (her word, not mine – I assumed it was tourism jargon for "getting off the bus"). We were to then direct them to the gambling casino or luncheon buffet depending on their preference.

As the first couple buses pulled in, I merely sat and watched as one of the more senior members of our team went to greet each. However, when the number of arriving buses exceeded the number of experienced staff members, I was directed to attend to the latest incoming bus. Thus began my livelihood as a "meet and greeter" as, I subsequently found, the position is known in the trade.

Not one with a problem speaking to anyone, I was relatively at ease in starting to read in deep and sonorous tones. That is, until the folks at the back of the bus began yelling.

Boisterous shouts of, "Can't hear you!" and, "Use the mike!" caromed off the interior of the bus. Suddenly, I was hit with stage fright. No one said anything about a microphone. Its appearance set to flight those butterflies hiding in my stomach.

Taking the instrument the bus driver thrust at me, I quickly put it to my mouth and recommenced my little speech. Not two lines into it and they were screaming, "Push in the button!" How did they all know how the stupid thing worked?

And if I could easily hear them, with my poor hearing, why did I need a microphone for them to hear me?! Anyway, once I mastered the high tech communications device (fighting the urge to end each section with, "Over and out") I managed to get through the itinerary and directions without any further problems.

Handing out the packages as they left the bus, I understood the significance of their groups' names. There were the Sunnyside Seniors, the Wolf Hill Red Hats, the Lonely Hearts of St. Mary's, and the Hibernian's Young at Hearts. Each traveler was well over seventy. The dance portion of the dinner show should be a real rocking event!

After tending to several more buses, I was given my best news yet of the day – we could partake of the buffet luncheon for free! We had a whole half-hour before our next duty, which was to set up the theater for that afternoon's show, *Christmas on Broadway*.

Knowing of my love of all buffets and my expertise in artfully navigating them, Adam assured me that I would not be disappointed. "The buffet is typical of most casinos – that is to say, it will be INCREDIBLY LARGE AND DIVERSE!!"

I was not disappointed.

Not one to stuff up on artificial fillers, I passed on the salads, breads, soups, and stuffed items (such as fish, peppers, and anything else into which you can shove rice or bread crumbs). I did a complete circumspection of the gourmet smorgasbord before starting to fill my plate. (Take note, those of you who are amateurs of the buffet world.)

And indeed, it was a wise decision, since just beyond the roasted meat carving station was the fresh seafood section! Shrimp as big as Italian sausages, crab legs that you could walk on, clams and oysters the size of Frisbees all called to me like a desert mirage beckons a man dying of thirst.

Having started out the day well before dawn with but a coffee and some donuts for sustenance, we did some serious damage to the buffet. My fellow staffers were in awe at the amount I could pile on a single plate. Indeed, the second and third trips to the serving bar, limited only by the short time we had, amazed them even further. The soft ice cream, topping a huge piece of cherry pie, was the perfect ending. I couldn't imagine what dinner would be like!

Setting up was rather uneventful since the hotel staff had taken care of most of it. I was tempted to return to the buffet, until Adam pointed to the crowd that was gathering outside the playhouse doors – a good half-hour before the scheduled opening, which was another half-hour before the show!

Adam explained that this is typical of the senior crowd. Regardless of any scheduled time they will appear, en masse, thirty minutes earlier and then complain that they are being forced to stand and wait. (I made a mental note to get to the next buffet a good forty minutes before the scheduled start.) We had to remain at the entrance to ward them off until they were allowed to enter.

Taking tickets at the door of the theater provided another opportunity to "meet and greet," but on a grander scale. With my large name tag, most of them felt we were now on a first name basis. I would live to regret this.

Our team next had to man tables in the lobby to distribute room keys to our guests. The hotel does not make them available upon arrival for fear they will hide in their rooms rather than gamble in the casinos. Thus, another opportunity to flash my name tag, with many of the ladies then providing me with their names and other unsolicited information such as their marital status! Though I noticed Adam getting some of the same attention, Carmella, Rosalie and the other elderly staffers were definitely not. I felt like I was being set up.

Completing that task just before five, I was then informed, much to my disappointment, that we were not to have dinner until after the guests' dinner show! (Another mental note: bulk up at the following day's luncheon buffet in light of this scheduling faux pas.) Instead, we were to assist the hotel staff in setting up the ballroom for the evening's entertainment. The itinerary listed it as beginning at seven o'clock, doors to open at six-thirty.

Scurrying around decorating the walls, placing center pieces, and setting up a Christmas tree was stressful but also fun. The waiters and waitresses were in good spirits, some even dancing in the aisles as the band got their sound systems set up. Then, at about six, I noticed the banquet hall's front doors beginning to "throb." Thinking a member of the staff was trying to come in, and not knowing only a single door was unlocked, I naively went over to let him, or her, in.

As I nudged open the huge door I was shocked to see over a hundred senior citizens, all dressed up for an evening out, standing in the lobby outside the ballroom waiting for the doors to open. I quickly closed the door only to see Carmella smiling and commenting about my making a "rookie mistake."

The doors were subsequently opened on schedule and a flood of humanity entered the banquet hall, each rushing to a pre-assigned table. Except that, most of them did not remember their assignment nor did they acknowledge how the tables were numbered. But rush in they did. Of course, I am being generous when I say "rush." Perhaps envision a NASCAR race, no, make that a Soap Box Derby with speed bumps.

After a considerable amount of relocation of rapidly seated citizenry, we got them all parked at their proper tables. Following another half-hour of grousing by the early birds, the meal was then wheeled out by the restaurant's staff. Carmella told me that my next job was to mingle among the tables over the next several hours to ensure that all was well.

MISTAKE!

I soon found that whenever you have a room full of senior citizens seated for a meal, at least half of them become gastronomic experts! Unsolicited critiques of the meal were tossed at me like free T-shirts at a basketball game. There were those who insisted on telling me that their meal was the worst they have ever had, said in a voice loud enough that those back in Brooklyn could hear. These were offset by those whispering that it was a meal worthy of a king.

The perfume wafting up from each table was overpowering. The fragrance industry must rely on Social Security to keep them afloat!! We could have reenacted the Nativity using live animals and not worry about anyone losing their appetite due to the smell of their "deposits."

As dinner wound down, with only a few returned meals, the dancing began. While there were some mixed couples, several pairs of women hit the floor. Watching from what I thought was afar, I was approached by a woman whose efforts to look "as young as a sixty-year-old" failed. Lifting my eyes to her, she was at least six-foot six, she asked me to dance – and the song was a slow one! I looked to Rosalie hoping for assurance that this was not in my contract. Getting nothing more than a smile for an answer, I accompanied my "date" to the floor.

Recalling the warnings of the nuns in junior high I made sure that a phone book could be placed between us as we fox-trotted our way across the floor. This was no small feat, as her strength was in direct proportion to her height.

Making small talk with Wanda was a challenge. I would relate what was said, but I don't remember a word exchanged. My mind was focused on not getting stepped on by this female version of Shrek. I feared for my life the whole time we were out there. (Cross off "professional dance partner" as a possible career.) Quickly exiting the floor after the song ended, I headed to an exit door lest there be any more requests for accompaniment.

Having revived myself in the lobby, I returned a short time later to join the staff at a table in the rear of the hall. After weathering their gibes, I heard about some little old lady who had been dancing a jitterbug and fell – landing flat on her back! As everyone on the dance floor gasped, the elderly matron broke out in raucous laughter and, much to everyone's surprise, spryly sprung to her feet.

As the end of the evening was nearing my colleagues and I were encouraged to resume our circulating to ensure that everyone was satisfied. Carefully avoiding Wanda, I was confronted by a small, feisty woman, who introduced herself as Francine. She insisted that I do a Rumba with her. (Yes, as it turned out, she was the same one who had fallen!)

Refusing to accept my claim that I could not do the Rumba, Francine dragged me out to the floor telling me to, "just follow." There were already two other couples on the floor, and they looked like they knew what they were doing.

Doing my best to not draw attention, we proceeded to do what looked like a mix of the Cha-cha and two people having just disrupted a wasp nest. Francine twirled and I smiled. Fortunately, Wanda did not take notice and the song ended relatively quickly with no one hitting the floor. (Must remember to cross off "professional dance partner" as a potential career with a very heavy pen.)

The following two days went in similar fashion. Each group came in for a single night. Of course, in addition to greeting new busloads, we had to ensure the proper departure of the prior day's guests. The latter task was somewhat difficult since so many treated us like old friends. Stopping just short of promising to "write soon," we bade them farewell and I headed back to the luncheon buffet in hopes that the shrimp was being frequently replenished!

Over the three days we met and greeted over a thousand people. Other than the dances with Wanda and Francine, the little whirling dervish, I was spared any further dances. Carmella and Rosalie promised to call me if they have any future opportunities for a seasoned "meet and greeter."

With regard to remuneration, Adam suggested, from experience, that if I had been a bit more available on the dance floor the tips could have been quite significant. Ugh, the thought of prostituting myself in that way...

Hmm, wonder if the Department of Labor has a detailed list of the duties of one whose job is to "meet and greet." If dance partnering is not included, I may have to reconsider – after all, the buffet was outstanding!

Man of Leisure

Ah, this career search can be exhausting, taxing the mind more than the body. And, yet, as I recall my career counselor's advice, it is important to keep physically fit as we seek out that which will occupy us in this next stage of our lives.

As the days have shortened so has my time spent exerting myself doing outdoor chores. Inversely, my time sitting in front of the PC has gotten greater as has the circumference of my waist. I need to find some form of exercise to address the latter.

Hmm, what form of exercise might take more time, not require a heavy amount of effort, and still provide the physical benefits that I seek?

GOLF!!

Yes, that sounds like the perfect solution. For years relegated to weekends due to my work schedule, it has continued that way for fear it would be a tacit acceptance of retirement and the associated lifestyle – after all, I am still actively seeking a new career! But now, viewed as an opportunity for exercise, rather than just a leisure activity, I will aggressively pursue it. I may even get my scores down to double digits.

Unlike many, my introduction to golf was relatively late in life. During my youth it was considered more of a wealthy man's game – we were more of the bowling and bocce ball set. Later, when friends were enticing me to join them at the course,

I was unable to justify the huge amount of time required to play a round, not willing to be away from our rapidly growing family for six hours on a weekend. Instead, I took up the game only when it became a career requirement.

Having reached the ranks of middle management, I found that the "gentleman's sport" was not the cricket of Rudyard Kipling, but another game that chased a smaller, though also white, ball. Golf was the common denominator of the titans of industry, and if I wanted to further my career it was important to take up the sport.

Looking back, I may have had better luck playing cricket.

My golf career got off to a less than auspicious start. Being alerted to the fact that an upcoming staff meeting was to be held at my boss' country club, I hastily acquired a beginner's set of clubs. I then went out to play a couple of weekend rounds with friends who had been playing since childhood. If not developing the skill that would result in low scores, I hoped to at least learn the etiquette, rules and, in an effort to distract from my lack of skill, some of the jargon used on the course.

"Worm burners" became the term assigned to my drives from the tee. My putting was compared to "shots from a cannon." I spent so much time in sand traps that they began to refer to me as "The Desert Fox." While becoming aware of the terms "par" and "bogey," I became intimate with "double-bogey" and "snowman." "Birdie" and "eagle" were to remain for me creatures that flew from tree to tree. It quickly became apparent that golf was going to be a formidable undertaking.

However, little did I know that my score at that now-infamous staff meeting would not be that which would be recalled by my colleagues for years to come.

Breakfast was the venue to address sufficient work issues to justify the outing as truly business-related – thus enabling the boss to get reimbursed for his expenses. Then, well before eleven, the eight of us headed to the clubhouse to pick up our clubs which had been dropped off upon our arrival. They awaited us like sentinels on duty upon racks adjacent to several motorized golf carts.

The boss had already ascertained everyone's skill level (or lack thereof) and assigned us to cart pairings based on handicaps. I was to accompany another golf "rookie."

An attendant offered to load our bags onto the carts. Already having dropped several bucks to have my car parked by a valet (a mere ten yards from the entrance), I was in no mood to continue to disburse greenbacks for something I could easily do myself. I made like I did not hear him and carried my clubs the fifteen feet to the cart, where I hoisted them onto the back. We then followed the others, lemming-like, to the first tee.

Concerned about too much separation if all of the big-hitters played together, the boss split the staff into two foursomes, each containing one cart with rookies or "high handicappers" as we became known. I was to be in the first foursome to tee off. The thought of the full group witnessing my feeble drive had the donuts from the morning's meeting reacquainting themselves with my upper digestive tract.

An elevated tee box overlooking a straight and very wide fairway provided some encouragement.

Leaving the cart parked at the crest of the slope, I approached the tee box in hopes that my drive would find some "air time" with the dramatic drop of the fairway.

The toss of a tee determined who would go first. Relieved, I found that I was to go last in our foursome. The two better golfers launched their shots into the horizon, only to land somewhere far down the fairway. My fellow beginner went next. Bob topped his shot, having it barely reach the left side of the slope in front of us which then mercifully enabled the ball to roll to the bottom – some fifty yards in front of the tee.

Approaching my ball to the sounds of tittering by the group behind us, I could feel the sweat dripping down my arms. (And this was supposed to be a bonding experience for the entire staff?) Carefully addressing the ball as I had seen the pros do on TV, I wound up for a mighty swing. Uncoiling in a fashion that had me envisioning my ball taking flight in a pattern similar to the first two of my playing partners, I looked up – only to see the ball make like a sled, not a plane, skidding down the slope to our right!

Not wanting to hear the laughter that was sure to follow, I quickly joined my partner in our cart and drove down to his ball. With the group continuing to watch our every move, Bob climbed out to hit his second shot. Miraculously, he managed to loft his shot into the air, the ball coming to a stop a good hundred yards farther down the fairway.

Anxious to make a similar escape from the scathing view of my boss and colleagues I spun the steering wheel of the cart hard to the right and hit the gas, heading toward my ball.

211

Arriving at it within seconds, I leapt out of the cart to retrieve the appropriate club from the rear of the cart. But, instead of finding my bag, full of clubs, standing on the cart – I found it hanging over the rear bumper with my clubs strewn across the fairway directly beneath the tee box.

Through the howling laughter of my colleagues I heard one of the more knowledgeable golfers cry out, "You forgot to strap your bag onto the cart!"

How was I to know? My first encounter with one of those stupid vehicles was when I put my bag on it some twenty minutes earlier. How I wished I had sprung for the couple bucks to have had the caddie load it!

Red-faced, I proceeded to pick up each of the twelve clubs that had fallen from the cart. At that point, I could have thrown each of those clubs further than the flag perched on the far distant green!

Not exactly the propitious start that I had envisioned for my golf career.

The years since that agonizing round have not seen much of an improvement in my game, though I have learned some important lessons. For one thing, I no longer use a mechanized cart, preferring instead to use a push cart – the walking provides more exercise. Also, I have found that the quality of the food and beverages accompanying each round is of greater import than the difficulty of the course. (My weekend rounds unfailingly start with a donut thanks to my buddy, Joe.) And lastly, whenever asked for my handicap, I now simply reply, "Depending on the day, either my driver or my putter!"

No longer is there a need to impress anyone in the company hierarchy. Heck, I can usually beat "the boss," (though it may be because she insists on hitting from the men's tees), and there is no one else here.

Now, golf is usually played in foursomes. Not really sure why, but those who assign you a tee time will do everything in their power to insert sufficient strangers into your group to ensure that there are at least three others witnessing your futile attempts to score well on your not-inexpensive excursion around the course.

Last Wednesday was the first of my new non-weekend exercise regimen. Joe, who also had taken an early retirement package, and I ventured out. Arriving at the course a good twenty minutes before our scheduled tee time, we gazed around the crowd to see who would be the two golfers joining us.

Might it be those two Asian women sitting in the golf cart, with the designer clubs and bags? Though often of small build, Asian women frequently are capable of driving the ball fifty yards beyond us – their precise swings demonstrating hours of expensive lessons!

Or might it be the two muscle-bound guys with the fire department logos on their T-shirts, enjoying one of their mid-week days off? Usually big hitters – the result not so much of lessons but from hours of pumping iron at the fire house.

Perhaps it would be one of the numerous old guys, invariably perched on their golf carts, incapable of walking the three and a half mile course, and waiting for a game. Not long ball hitters with their restricted swings, they are often incredibly accurate thus achieving very low scores – the result of having played so many years they remember guys with cool

213

names like Slammin' Sammy Snead and Ben "The Hawk" Hogan.

At last, the starter called out our names and those of two others – Jeffrey and Nigel.

Meeting up with them at the first tee box, we introduced ourselves. Jeffrey turned out to be an Asian man, who did not speak English. (Something led me to suspect that "Jeffrey" was not his real name.) He bowed to us and we returned the greeting. Those were the last words exchanged for the next four hours – we did compliment several of his strokes, each of which was answered with a modest, though silent bow.

Our other partner for the day, Nigel, turned out to be a British fellow, living here in the States on a holiday visa. His was an interesting story.

An architect by profession, he had accompanied his wife, an international banker, who was on a two year assignment in New York City. Not allowed to accept employment under the conditions of his visa, he was a self-described "man of leisure." He went on to further explain in a delightfully accented voice, "What is known more popularly here in the colonies as a *kept man*." Thus, he was now just enjoying life during his time here.

He then turned the attention to me. "And what is it that you do, old chap?"

I immediately dropped all pretense of being a leisurely golfer and went into a brief encapsulation of my business résumé. "Following a lengthy career in Finance with a Fortune 100 company, I took an early retirement offer. I'm now doing some programming and consulting work while actively seeking a second career." Confident that I had delivered a successfully modified version of my "two minute intro," I was surprised by his reaction.

"What is it with you Americans? One never simply retires or leaves a job – you all seem to become 'consultants'! It is my belief that you, like me, are indeed a 'man of leisure'. You should graciously accept the mantle that has been thrust upon you by the lords of industry." (You have to love the way the British turn a phrase – that is if you can understand their accent.)

Quickly recovering from his assessment, I turned toward my buddy and said, "Ah, have you met Joe?"

Fortunately, Joe tends to understand the Queen's English, as well as most other foreign accents, sufficiently well to participate in any required conversation during our oft-multinational rounds of golf. I, on the other hand, require subtitles when watching movies featuring actors from the British realm.

I think I heard Joe say something about being on "sabbatical." Then, rather than getting into a career discussion, he quickly proceeded to comment on the exquisite set of clubs Nigel had in his bag. Must remember to compliment Joe on his tap dancing skills.

The round went well. I avoided the temptation to pitch my consulting services, instead focusing on my golf and the exercise it was providing. Joe maintained the golf-centric patter with Nigel. Jeffrey was clearly the best of the group – arriving on the greens with the fewest strokes and invariably insisting that we all tee off before him. Not sure if that is what he was saying, but we would each tee off while he was still bowing.

215

Nigel, in spite of his expensive-looking clubs, displayed a talent for golf that might enable him to drive carts, not golf balls, at the next British Open. Joe and I made an honest effort to break into double digits, and would have done so had we quit after the sixteenth hole. Ah well, so golf may not be a viable option for my next livelihood.

However, golf is not what is on my mind today – rather, the words spoken by Nigel at the first tee. They have been ringing in my ears ever since, and I have elected to seriously consider this as a career option. I am even thinking of having business cards printed up in which my title would be "Man of Leisure." I could hand them out to cashiers at the supermarket, little old ladies doing battle with me over the plum tomatoes at the vegetable stand, and the guy at the tool rental agency.

Thus, today is the first business day of operating under my new title. Wonder if I will have to wear those funny looking suits that were all the rage in the disco era of the seventies? At least they did not warrant wearing a tie. But the day has not gotten off to a rousing start...

Having finished a brief programming job last Friday, today I was prepared to attack my career as a "Man of Leisure" in earnest. Always wanting to be helpful, "the boss" had some suggestions for initiating that objective. They were detailed on an updated "Honey Do" list.

The first item was, "Clean up that pigsty you call an office." (When it was a toy room it was acceptable to have all kinds of junk on the floor. What a difference a name change makes.) Next came, "Bundle the newspapers for the trash pickup."

(Remember when we could just dump them in with the rest of the garbage? Now with "recycling" we must tie them with a string and bow to enable them to be picked up at curbside.) Directives to make a delivery of outgrown clothes (thank you, South Beach Diet) to a local charity, and I think I saw a reference to placing a phone in my office (something about my tendency to allow calls go to voicemail when I am the only one home) rounded out the list.

This "Man of Leisure" idea is draining me and it is not even ten o'clock! Wonder what Nigel is doing today?

Well, I will get to each of those items on the "Honey Do" list in due course. If nothing else, I am diligent about my duties in whatever livelihood I happen to be pursuing.

But first, let me pull up the ESPN website to see who won yesterday's Senior's Tour golf tournament. It is important for a man in my position to be familiar with such statistics in the event I run into someone in a similar career – beyond sports what else is there to discuss? Indeed, if the scores of those on the leader board are near three digits, I might reconsider my decision to not pursue a career in golf.

Until that or another opportunity arises, I will just have to accept my status in life as a "Man of Leisure."

ABOUT THE AUTHOR

 Since the age of three, Jerry Della Rocca had worn a tie from 8-5, Monday through Friday. With little warning, the company where he worked for over thirty years offered him "a package too good to be true" (his employer's words) and he accepted early-retirement.

He now lives and writes on Long Island, NY with the love of his life, Elise. He's never written for Atlantic Monthly, Esquire, or Vanity Fair. He has never won any major literary awards, though his sixth-grade essay entitled "My Best Sundae Ever" did win him a prize in Dairy Queen's Summer of '59 campaign – he's still waiting to hear from the Pulitzer Committee.

A life-long story teller blessed with many a misadventure, he's never lacked for an anecdote about time spent in the wrong life lane. Now, as he ventures into an unplanned and unanticipated life of pre-mature retirement, he continues to share tales of his adventures at finding a new passion to fill forty hours a week.

Printed in Great Britain
by Amazon.co.uk, Ltd.,
Marston Gate.